MATT CHRISTOPHER

On the Field with...

MATT CHRISTOPHER

On the Field with...

Mia Hamm

Little, Brown and Company
Boston   New York   London

Second Paperback Edition

Library of Congress Cataloging-in-Publication Data

Christopher, Matt.
    On the field with — Mia Hamm / Matt Christopher.
       p.   cm.
    Summary: A biography of one of the top female soccer players in the country, Mia Hamm, who helped the United States win a gold medal in soccer in the 1996 Olympics.
    ISBN 0-316-13484-8 (pb)
    1. Hamm, Mia, 1972–   — Juvenile literature.   2. Women soccer players — United States — Biography — Juvenile literature.
[1. Hamm, Mia, 1972–   . 2. Soccer players. 3. Women — Biography.] I. Title.
GV942.7.H27C57   1998
796.334'092 — dc21
[b]   98-14937

10 9 8 7 6 5 4 3 2 1

COM-MO

Printed in the United States of America

Contents

MATT CHRISTOPHER

On the Field with...

Mia Hamm

Prologue

On the afternoon of August 1, 1996, more than seventy-six thousand spectators poured into Sanford Stadium on the campus of the University of Georgia in Athens, Georgia. There was nothing unique about that. The University of Georgia football team, the Bulldogs, regularly drew that many fans to each of their home football games every season.

But football wasn't the reason the stadium was full that day. People from all over the world had come to Athens for just one reason. They wanted to see the United States women's soccer team, led by Mia Hamm, play the women's team from the People's Republic of China. Millions more were watching on television. At stake that afternoon was an Olympic gold medal — the first ever — in women's soccer.

Never before had so many people gathered to watch a women's sporting event.

Only a few decades earlier, the notion that so many people would watch a soccer game played by women had been inconceivable. Women competed in only a select few sports, such as track and field, golf, tennis, gymnastics, basketball, and figure skating. Many people thought sports like soccer were simply too physically demanding for women to play. Sports were for boys. Girls were supposed to stand on the sidelines and cheer.

Although soccer was the most popular sport in the world and was becoming increasingly popular in the United States as a children's sport, only a few women in the entire world played competitive soccer. Those that did played in obscurity. Few people even knew that women played soccer. In the United States only a few high schools had a women's soccer team. Not until 1978 did a single college or university have a varsity women's soccer program! There was no such thing as a national team or Women's World Cup competition. No one dreamed that women would someday play soccer in the Olympics.

That was all about to change.

Chapter One:
1972–1976

Chasing the Ball

One day in 1973, on the sidelines of a soccer field in Italy, a young American girl sat with her family and watched two teams of Italian boys play soccer. No one in the family understood the game very well, but they still enjoyed watching the two teams race back and forth across the field, controlling the ball with their feet with as much skill and mastery as a basketball player handles the basketball or a hockey player the puck.

The shy young girl, just over a year old and barely able to walk, seemed particularly enthralled. Standing close to her parents, she never took her eyes off the black-and-white soccer ball. Whenever the ball bounded off the field in her direction, she giggled and toddled away from her parents, chasing after it along with other children in the crowd and trying to kick it like the players on the field.

She didn't know that girls weren't supposed to play sports. For her, it was fun to chase after the ball and kick it, to run around with other children, then sit and play in the grass together, making friends.

That's how Mia Hamm's soccer career began. Years later, her love of the sport and the friendships she made on the field would take her all over the world.

Mariel Margaret Hamm was born on March 17, 1972, in Selma, Alabama. Her father, William, was a pilot in the United States Air Force, and her mother, Stephanie, was a ballerina. Soon after she was born, her mother started calling her Mia, because the baby reminded her of a ballet teacher with the same name.

As a member of the air force, Bill Hamm was never stationed in one place for very long. In 1973, he was transferred to Italy. The entire family, which then also included an older brother and two older sisters, accompanied Bill to Florence, Italy.

When he wasn't flying airplanes, Bill Hamm loved

to watch sports. But in Italy, hardly anyone played the sports Bill watched in the United States, such as baseball and football and basketball. The biggest game in Italy was soccer.

No matter where the family went, it seemed as if a soccer game was being played. In almost every open field or empty street, gangs of young boys raced after a soccer ball. Virtually every town had a men's team, and larger cities often supported several soccer clubs. Most teams were amateur, but the Italians also sponsored several thriving professional leagues. Thousands of fans turned out to support their favorite team, chanting and singing in unison in the stands and waving huge flags and banners. Televised soccer games were the most popular programs in the country.

When Bill started watching soccer, he didn't understand the game very well. Soccer wasn't popular in the United States. Only a few public schools and colleges had soccer teams. There was a professional league, the North American Soccer League, but few people went to the games and they were rarely televised. Only a handful of the players were from the

United States. Most were from Europe and South America. In the United States, Bill hadn't paid attention to the game.

But in Italy, he had little choice. If he wanted to watch sports, he had to watch soccer. And the more he watched, the more he began to appreciate the sport. He realized that what had first looked to him like a bunch of players randomly running after a ball was actually a sport that demanded great athletic skill and strategy. He learned that every player on the team played a specific position, just as in basketball or hockey, and had different responsibilities. The more Bill learned about the game, the more he enjoyed it. Soon, he was a rabid soccer fan.

The family loved to do things together, and Bill started taking his family to soccer games. The children, particularly Mia, took to the game immediately. She was small for her age and usually quite shy. But when she saw a soccer ball, her eyes lit up. On the air force base, she often joined other children in impromptu games of soccer.

After only a few years in Italy, Bill was transferred again, this time back to the United States. Although the family left Italy behind, they took their love of soccer with them. They spent a brief period in California, then Bill was sent to Wichita Falls, Texas.

When they arrived there, Bill and Stephanie Hamm were pleased to learn that the community supported a youth soccer program. Little League baseball and other youth sports programs like Pop Warner football were commonplace, but youth soccer programs were still rare in the United States.

Yet ever so slowly, the sport was becoming more and more popular. Unlike many other sports, soccer doesn't require a great deal of equipment. It is relatively safe for children even as young as five or six years old to play. The basics of the game are easy to learn. If you can run and kick a ball, you can play. And one of the best things about soccer is that every player gets to touch the ball.

Because soccer is a sport that relies more on speed and agility than strength and size, soccer is one of the few sports that allows boys and girls to play together. Kids of similar ages, both male and female, are able to compete equally. Actually, since young girls mature faster than boys, girls are often the better players.

When Mia's older sisters and brother found out

7

there was a league in town, they wanted to play. Bill was delighted and did his best to support his children. Although he was still learning the game himself, he started studying the rules and fundamentals of the game. He became a coach and referee so he could learn even more and make sure his children learned how to play correctly. He studied every book about soccer he could find.

At first, Mia wasn't allowed to play on a team. She was still too young. Yet the family spent most of just about every Saturday at the soccer field. Mia loved watching her siblings and the other kids play. Every time an errant kick came her way, she was off and running after it. Her mother often spent most of her Saturdays chasing after Mia!

Mia's mother recognized that her daughter was full of energy and thought she might enjoy taking ballet lessons, just as she herself had when she was a young girl. So when Mia turned five, her mother enrolled her in a dancing class. "She was so petite, I thought she'd be ideal," her mother later said.

That's not quite the way it turned out. As far as Mia was concerned, dance class was too slow. It seemed that as soon as everyone in class started moving, the teacher would have everyone stop to learn something else. Besides, Mia didn't like wearing ballet slippers. As she told a reporter years later, "I hated it. I lasted only one class."

Mia wanted to play soccer, as her brother and sisters did. Her mother understood. She remembered that when she was growing up, there were few opportunities for girls to play sports. As she later recalled, "Those of us who wanted to be active found the joy in using our body in something like dance. Now they have this other option and it's beautiful." She put Mia's ballet shoes in a closet and bought her a tiny pair of soccer cleats and shin guards.

At age five, Mia joined an organized team. She was one of the smallest and youngest players on the team.

But that didn't stop Mia. She had grown up with the game and played a lot with her older sisters and brother. She understood how the game was supposed to be played. Although she was timid at first, she quickly discovered that as soon as she started scoring goals, she didn't feel so shy anymore. As she remembered later, "Soccer was a way to hang out and make friends."

In time, it would become much more than that.

Chapter Two:
1977–1986

Choosing Soccer

The opportunity to play organized soccer wasn't the only event of 1977 that had a significant impact on Mia's life. The Hamm family expanded by one when her parents adopted a Thai-American orphan, an eight-year-old boy named Garrett.

Soon, Mia and Garrett were nearly inseparable. He, too, loved to play soccer and other sports. "He was an instant playmate for me," she remembers.

As Mia grew up, she tried to do everything Garrett did. "He let me hang out with him and his friends and play football, soccer, and basketball with them," she says.

Despite her small size, Mia was a good athlete. Garrett knew this, and called his little sister his "secret weapon."

Garrett and Mia would join his friends in the park

for pickup games of baseball, football, basketball, and soccer. "No one would want to pick me for their team," says Mia, "but Garrett would always pick me. We would downplay the fact that I was fast and could catch."

But then, at a critical moment in the game, Garrett and Mia would give each other a look. All of a sudden, Mia would start playing hard, running as fast as she could. Usually she left her opponents far behind, racing in to kick a goal in soccer or catching a long touchdown pass.

Playing against older kids helped Mia quickly improve her skills. Soon she wasn't a secret weapon anymore. The neighborhood kids knew she was an athlete to be reckoned with.

In 1982, when Mia was ten years old, the most important soccer competition in the world, the World Cup, was played in Spain. Every four years, nearly every nation on earth selects a national soccer team. Over the course of a year they play in regional tournaments to qualify for World Cup competition, a final round made up of the best sixteen teams in the world. The sixteen teams play against one another until only two teams remain. Those two teams then compete for the world championship of soccer, the World Cup.

Although more and more children were playing soccer, very few Americans paid much attention to the 1982 World Cup. Except for a brief period in the mid-1970s, when the Brazilian superstar Pelé briefly played in the North American Soccer League, soccer had never been a popular spectator sport in America.

The American national team hadn't even qualified for the World Cup final round since 1950. Most Americans didn't know the United States even had a national team, much less what the World Cup was. The United States was about the only country in the world that didn't televise the event. Everywhere else, the World Cup was like the Super Bowl, the World Series, the NBA Finals, and the Stanley Cup all wrapped up in one event. Billions of people worldwide watched the finals on television.

Living in Wichita Falls, near the American-Mexican border, the Hamm family could pick up Mexican television broadcasts. In Mexico, soccer was extremely popular. The World Cup was huge. Television stations broadcast almost every game of the final rounds of the tournament, even when they took place on the other side of the world in the middle of the night.

The Hamm family watched as many games as they possibly could. Even though the announcers broadcast the games in Spanish, everyone in the family understood the game. As they watched the best players in the world, they discussed strategy and marveled at their skill. When they had a chance, Mia and the other Hamm children would race outside and try to imitate the players they had just watched.

The 1982 World Cup, which Italy won, defeating West Germany 3–1 in the final game, was an important event in Mia's life. She began to realize how the game of soccer was meant to be played and what it was possible to do with a soccer ball. Furthermore, she became aware of just how big and important soccer was. It could be more than a game she played in order to hang out with her friends. She didn't yet pay much attention to the fact that every team in the World Cup was all-male. She just knew she could hardly wait for the next World Cup to be played.

But Mia wasn't quite ready to turn her life over to

soccer. After all, she was still a kid and enjoyed lots of different sports. She was good at every sport she chose to play, and she tried to play everything, even becoming one of the first girls in Wichita Falls to play Little League. She didn't know it, but she was a pioneer.

She even played football. When Mia was in seventh grade, a bunch of her friends were all excited about trying out for the school's junior high football team. They had all played football together on the playground. Mia knew she could throw and kick a football as well as any of her friends, male or female, and no one could run as fast as she could. When tryouts were announced, Mia signed up without hesitation.

She had never noticed that girls didn't usually play football. Not until she went to practice did she realize that she was the only girl trying to make the team. "It was one of those things when you're young," she said later. "You really don't think boy-girl. They were my friends. They wanted me to play."

Being the only female trying out didn't stop her. Her friends told the coach she was a good player.

It didn't take long for the coach to learn that Mia's friends were right. She made the team easily. She tried quarterback but usually played wide receiver and kicked.

But as Mia grew older, it became increasingly apparent that her best sport was soccer. "I found I cared more about the results in soccer than in any other sport," she said. And as her male friends kept growing, Mia began to realize that she was just too small to keep playing football. She was a good basketball player and baseball player, an asset to the teams she played for. But on the soccer field, she was a star.

Mia usually played forward. On offense, she'd streak down the sideline after the ball, then either pass to a teammate or break out toward the goal herself. When the other team had the ball, she usually formed the first line of defense. In order to move the ball past midfield and get in position to score, the opposition first had to get the ball past Mia.

For many young athletes, the most difficult part about any sport is learning to anticipate, to see what is happening on the field before it actually happens. Because she played so much while so young, Mia developed that skill while still a child. While most of her peers were still trying to figure out how to run full speed and control the ball at the same time, Mia did all that instinctively. She could concentrate on the mental part of the game instead. Before she even got the ball, she was thinking a play or two ahead of her teammates. When the ball reached her, she usually knew what she was going to do with it. If the defense slacked off her, anticipating a pass, she knew to go on the attack and charge the goal. If they covered her closely, she seemed to know instinctively where her teammates were and how to get them the ball.

The opposition soon learned that if they didn't pay attention to Mia, she could score at will. Two or three players were often assigned to cover her the entire game.

But that didn't stop Mia. She realized that if two or three players were covering her, a teammate or two had to be wide open. One of her favorite tricks was to run across the middle of the field with the ball to force several defenders to race after her. When they did, she'd spin and make a perfect pass between them to a wide-open teammate in front of the goal.

She was so quick to the ball and so alert on the field that it almost appeared as if she was playing a different game. By the time she became a teenager, she had graduated from the local youth leagues to club teams made up of the best players from several communities. She also played on her school team, at Notre Dame High School in Wichita Falls. She stopped playing other sports and concentrated on soccer.

As the competition improved, so did Mia. She quickly developed from being just one of the best players in Wichita Falls to being the very best, then to one of the best players in the state.

Yet Mia didn't get a big head. She really didn't care whether she scored or not, as long as her team won.

Meanwhile, nationwide, women's soccer, and women's sports in general, were getting bigger. Throughout the 1970s and early 1980s, people began to realize that women had just as much of a right to play sports as men and that there was no physical reason for them not to play. The United States government even recognized that fact and ruled that school sports programs had to treat male and female athletes equally. That regulation, known as Title IX, spurred many high schools and colleges to expand their sports programs for girls and women.

Many high schools began to sponsor women's soccer teams, as did many colleges. Women were even being offered scholarships to college to play soccer. Beginning in 1982, the National Collegiate Athletic Association, or NCAA, started a collegiate national championship tournament. That same year, the United States selected its first national women's soccer team to compete internationally.

The United States was finally catching up to the rest of the world. In most European countries women's soccer had already been an established sport for a decade or more. Millions of young girls and women around the world now played soccer, and thousands more were beginning to play each year.

Mia Hamm began playing soccer at just the right time, when opportunities for women soccer players were expanding rapidly. Women's soccer groups were talking about someday holding a women's

World Cup tournament, and there was a growing movement to include women's and men's soccer in the Olympic Games.

In 1985, when Mia was just thirteen years old, she was a Texas All-State selection in women's soccer. The selection qualified her to play in several big tournaments and all-star games.

At one such game, John Cossaboon, coach of the fledgling United States women's soccer Olympic development team, was watching the game. He wasn't really scouting for his own team, but was looking for good players he could recommend to college coaches, where he hoped they would develop into good players. Cossaboon attended dozens of games each year.

As soon as he started watching, he couldn't take his eyes off Mia Hamm. She was all over the field, stripping the ball from her opponents on defense and dominating play on offense, setting up her teammates with perfect passes and making aggressive moves to the goal. After only a few moments, it became obvious to Cossaboon that even on a team of all-stars, she stood out. No one else on the field had her speed or feel for the game.

And she was tough, too! Where other players sometimes hesitated to make a tackle or tried to avoid contact, Mia played hard but clean. She didn't think twice about running headlong into a crowd for the ball. Her desire often allowed her to win balls from players who had much better position.

Cossaboon couldn't believe it when he learned that Mia was only thirteen. She was the youngest player on the field and already the best player. By his standards, she was still a little raw and had lots to learn, but she had potential to burn.

When Cossaboon looked at Mia, he saw the future of women's soccer in the United States. Without hesitation, he asked Mia to join the Olympic development team. He told her parents that Mia was already good enough to get a college scholarship.

Mia was dumbfounded. She had never really thought about playing soccer much beyond high school, let alone someday having a chance to play in the Olympic Games. Now, all of a sudden, she knew what she wanted to do.

She wanted to be a soccer player. No one could tell her sports were just for boys.

Chapter Three:
1987

A Member of the Team

When Mia joined the Olympic development team, her life changed. Before, soccer simply had been a game she played and enjoyed. Now, next to her family, it was the most important thing in her life.

Being a member of the team gave Mia a chance to travel all around the country and play soccer with the best young American players. Some girls her age might have had a difficult time doing that without getting homesick. But Mia was prepared. Her family had moved several times as she was growing up, so she was accustomed to meeting new people and adjusting to new situations. She was still shy but had learned that soccer was a good way to make friends.

Once again, the stronger the competition she faced, the better she seemed to play. After only one year with Mia on his team, Coach Cossaboon knew that it would soon be time for Mia to move on. She was improving rapidly, and he wanted to make sure she was allowed to reach her full potential.

Cossaboon contacted Anson Dorrance, coach of both the University of North Carolina women's soccer team and the United States national team. He told Dorrance that he had a player that he just had to see.

In the world of American women's soccer, Dorrance was famous. On the UNC campus in Chapel Hill, North Carolina, he was as admired as Dean Smith, the legendary coach of the men's basketball team. Smith even admitted as much, once telling an out-of-town reporter that the basketball team wasn't such a big deal around Chapel Hill, because UNC "was really a girls soccer school."

Dorrance had attended and played for UNC, and he began his collegiate coaching career with the UNC men's team in 1976, a position he held through 1989. When UNC decided to create a varsity women's team in 1979, Dorrance took on that task as well.

Dorrance was a tough taskmaster who demanded results. At first, he tried to coach the women just as he did the men. He soon learned that didn't work very well.

Dorrance eventually came to the conclusion that he had to take a different approach to the women's team. Women players, he discovered, had to trust him before they would carry out his instructions.

He stopped yelling so much and started teaching. "With women, if you want to get the most out of them, they have to feel you relate personally to them," he later told an interviewer. Once that took place, Dorrance discovered that "there is a genuine team cohesiveness among great women's teams because they have a greater capacity to relate to each other than we do as males."

Before long, his women's team was even more successful than his men's squad. Dorrance enjoyed his new task so much that he eventually gave up his post as men's coach to coach the women's team full-time. Under his tutelage, the UNC women's team became a dynasty.

They rarely lost a game. In 1982 they captured the first NCAA women's soccer championship and in the ensuing five seasons won four more titles. In 1986, based on his unparalleled record of success,

Dorrance was also named coach of the United States women's national team. No one in the country knew more about women's soccer, and women soccer players, than Dorrance.

Although women's soccer was much more established in Europe, Asia, and South America, Dorrance set out to create the best women's soccer team in the world. His position as national team coach gave him the opportunity to see the best women soccer players in the world. He knew that if the United States was ever going to compete at the international level, he had to have the best players on his team. He traveled the country in search of those select few young women.

Yet no young player he had seen before made as strong an impression on him as Mia Hamm. He got his first look at Mia in 1987, when she played for an under-19 team at a national tournament in New Orleans, Louisiana. Watching her closely from the sidelines, Dorrance later remembered, "She was playing right halfback. I watched her take a seven-yard run at the ball, and I said, 'Oh, my gosh!' I'd never seen speed like that in the women's game. She had unlimited potential. . . . She had an incredible ability to shred defenders and get to the goal."

Like Cossaboon, Dorrance wanted to make sure that soccer remained a challenge to Mia, so she would continue to make the most of her ability. For despite her obvious skill and talent, at the international level the game was far different from the one Mia had been playing. Thus far, she had relied on her physical ability to succeed against players who were less talented and experienced.

But in international play, every player was fast and strong, and many had more experience than Mia. In order to make certain her game continued to develop to its full potential, Dorrance realized he had to expose Mia to the level of play practiced by the United States national team. He asked her to participate in an upcoming training camp and try out for the team. Even if she didn't make it, she would learn what it would take for her game to reach the next level.

Mia agreed. She was excited by the opportunity Dorrance provided, but she was also apprehensive. Most other team members were either in college or had recently graduated. Mia Hamm was only fifteen years old.

She was nervous, shy, and a little intimidated. All of a sudden, she was supposed to play with players such as striker Michelle Akers, who many people considered to be the best women's soccer player in the world. At Mia's first meeting with the team, they all spent several hours in the gym, working out with weights and other fitness equipment.

Mia had never spent much time in the gym before. She'd just played soccer. The long workout left her exhausted. "I thought I'd die," she remembered later.

Then she got the surprise of her young life. After working out in the gym, the squad headed outside for practice! She spent another two hours on the field, going through drills and scrimmages with the team. At the end of the day, all she wanted to do was sleep. Her thighs throbbed, and she felt as if her entire body was going to go into one huge cramp. She had never worked so hard in her life.

Yet she couldn't keep her eyes closed. Every time she did, she saw herself playing soccer on the national team. She was more excited about the game than she had ever been before. The players on the team were so good, they made Mia reassess her entire approach to soccer.

The experience made a lasting impression on Mia. Thus far, soccer had been important to her and she had cared about winning or losing, but she had never felt that losing was the end of the world. As a female athlete, she had been conditioned to care less about winning than male athletes did.

On the national team, everything was different. "I loved how competitive it was," she said later. "I was like, 'Wow. Look how hard these players work.'" The captain of the national team, April Heinrichs, made a particular impression on Hamm. "She just wanted to win, and for a female wanting that, it was just so new. I realized I had to do a lot of stuff on my own if I wanted to stay on this team."

Mia was also astounded by their grasp of the game. As she later recalled, she realized that "tactically, I didn't have a clue. I had no idea how to play," at least at the international level. She knew little about the subtleties of strategy and playing together as a team with players who were as skilled as she was.

When she returned home after the camp, she was one hundred percent committed to playing soccer. She knew exactly what she wanted out of the game of soccer. "She came back from camp," said her father, "and said she wanted to do two things. Go to North Carolina [to play for Dorrance at UNC] and win the world championship." She had become best friends with one of her teammates on the under-19 team, Kristine Lilly, and the two girls dreamed of going off together to UNC and playing on the national team.

Mia's dream soon started to come true. Dorrance named her to the U.S. team. In August of 1987, Mia accompanied the squad to China, where they were scheduled to play two games against the Chinese national team.

Even for an experienced traveler like Mia, the trip to China was still a big deal. But Mia was most excited about getting an opportunity to play with the U.S. team. She made her first appearance for the United States in the first game against China, on August 3, 1987, in Tianjin. There were thousands of fans in the stands, more than Mia had ever played for before.

She didn't start but entered the game as a substitute. She was so nervous, her few moments on the field went by in a blur. While she was confident in her skills on offense, she wasn't so sure about her defensive play. On the international level, defense is vital. Because all the players are so talented, a single goal is often the difference in a game. Mia was still learning her defensive responsibilities and didn't feel confident.

All she could think about was trying not to screw up. And although she didn't score a goal or play particularly well, she didn't screw up, either. She had survived her first game in international competition. The United States won, 2–0.

At the time, Mia was what coaches sometimes refer to as a "project," a player with vast potential who needs time to learn and develop. Coach Dorrance, although he wanted to win every game the team played, was already looking toward the future. In a few years, he hoped that FIFA, the international organization that runs soccer, would agree to hold a women's World Cup competition. Dorrance knew that by the time that took place, some of his best players on the current team would likely be gone, lost to either retirement or injury. He needed young players like Mia to start learning his system now, so that if a women's World Cup was ever held, they would be ready to contribute. He knew it would take time for Mia to become a force on the team.

In the meantime, Mia still had to finish high school. After all, she was only in the tenth grade.

After her sophomore year, her father gathered the family and told them some important news. Bill Hamm, who was now a colonel in the air force, was being transferred again. The Hamm family would have to move from Texas to northern Virginia.

It was a stressful time for everyone in the family. A few years before, Mia's brother Garrett had been diagnosed with a disease called aplastic anemia, a blood disorder that caused his body to fail to produce enough platelets. Garrett, whom Mia had always looked up to and considered the best athlete in the family, had to stop playing sports. Although he continued to lead an almost normal life, the malady was progressive and a source of constant concern.

Mia didn't know what to think about the transfer to northern Virginia. Although she was accustomed to moving around a lot, she didn't want to leave all her friends at school and have to start all over again. Then she realized that the move to northern Virginia would bring her closer to the other members of the national team, many of whom also played for Dorrance at the University of North Carolina. She probably wouldn't have to spend as much time away from her family as before. Besides, as the child of a parent in the military, Mia knew the routine.

"You move and have new friends as soon as you join a team," she says. In the years ahead, she would be making friends all over the world.

Chapter Four:

1988-1989

From Shooting Star to Tar Heel

The Hamms moved to Burke, Virginia, in time for Mia to enroll in Lake Braddock High School in the fall of 1988. Once they got settled, the family quickly discovered that northern Virginia and the suburbs around Washington, D.C., were a hotbed of women's soccer. It didn't take long for Mia Hamm to find a new team. In fact, she joined two teams.

Lake Braddock High had a strong soccer program. In 1987 the girls team won the Virginia AAA state championship. In the spring of 1988, they were heavily favored to repeat, but lost in overtime to arch rival Woodbridge in the finals.

The school's academic program was just as important to Mia. She knew that the national team would soon take up a great deal of her time. So after discussing it with her parents and the administration at

Lake Braddock High, she decided to accelerate her academic program and simultaneously complete both her junior and senior years. The fact that Coach Dorrance had offered her a scholarship to play soccer at UNC was another incentive for her to complete her high school education. She couldn't wait to get there.

But soccer was a spring sport in Virginia, so in the meantime Mia joined a club team, the Braddock Road Shooting Stars, one of the best junior girls soccer clubs in the country. Several of her teammates from Lake Braddock were also on the squad.

It was a hectic year. Mia spent most of her time studying, working out, and playing soccer. Unlike many girls her age, she rarely dated or attended dances. There just wasn't enough time.

When spring came, she joined the Lake Braddock girls soccer team, the Bruins. They were already favored to win the state championship.

By this time, Mia was no secret to other teams in northern Virginia. Her notoriety as a member of the national team and performance on the Shooting Stars had marked her as one of the best soccer players in the state. Bruins Coach Carolyn Rice looked forward to having such a talented player join her team.

Coming in new to an established team can be an unnerving experience. Sometimes, established players resent new players, particularly those as talented as Mia. Although Mia was looking forward to playing, she knew it might not be easy at first. The Bruins were already loaded with talent. Eight of eleven starters had returned from the previous season. Even though she knew several teammates from the Shooting Stars and had met everyone else during her first semester at Lake Braddock, she still worried about fitting in.

When practice started, Coach Rice and the Bruin players soon discovered that Mia was an even better player than they had thought. But they learned that the best part about having Mia on the team wasn't the way she played. It was the way she acted.

"The thing that stands out about Mia," Coach Rice later told a reporter, "is her attention to the details of every task. She works hard to push herself, but by her own actions, she also motivates and encourages the others to work even harder."

Mia didn't have an attitude. If anything, she

downplayed her own accomplishments and was modest to a fault. Her experience with the national team had taught her the importance of team chemistry. Before long, her teammates didn't look at her as someone new. She had become their friend, and a teammate in every sense of the word.

Coach Rice installed Mia on the team's forward line with two established star players, Collette Cunningham and Liz Pike. Soon the three talented girls were the scourge of women's soccer in the state of Virginia.

Despite the fact that every opponent was gunning for the Bruins, they raced through the bulk of their season undefeated. But late in the year, they stumbled, losing games to Woodson and West Springfield.

As Coach Rice commented later, the losses only made the Bruins more determined to win the state championship. "They knew what they did wrong," she said at the time. "I didn't have to tell them."

In their last few regular season games, the team got back on track and qualified for the state tournament. In the semifinals, Mia scored two goals in a 5–1 win over Monacan. That set up a rematch between Lake Braddock and Woodbridge in the finals on May 27.

Woodbridge assigned their best defender, Susan Braun, to cover Mia. Although Braun wasn't as quick as Mia, she was a smart player who wisely worked hard to keep Mia's teammates from getting her the ball.

But no one on the field had Mia's skills and experience. She made the most of her few opportunities.

Fourteen minutes into the game, the score was 0–0. Then Mia got free.

With the ball near midfield and Woodbridge on the attack, a Lake Braddock player stole the ball. Without hesitating, Mia raced toward the Woodbridge goal, looking for the ball.

Her quick burst took Braun by surprise, and Mia's teammate hit her with a perfect pass. Mia dribbled quickly downfield. Only one defender stood between her and the goalkeeper.

As Coach Dorrance had previously noticed, no one got by defenders better than Mia. She raced straight toward the Woodbridge player, then faked and cut to the side, leaving the befuddled girl stumbling and trying to change direction. By the time she did, Mia was already several yards past her and in the clear.

Woodbridge goalie Erin Tierney had no chance. From just outside the penalty box, Mia blasted a shot past her outstretched arms into the right corner of the net. She was quickly surrounded by her cheering teammates. Lake Braddock led, 1–0.

But Woodbridge fought back. Over the next twenty minutes, neither team scored as Braun recovered to hold Mia in check.

Then, at the forty-one-minute mark, Mia got the ball again deep in Lake Braddock territory on the right side.

The sight of Mia Hamm with the ball so close to the goal alarmed the Woodbridge defense. Another player joined Braun, and they tried to force Mia into the corner.

That was a mistake. Mia knew that somewhere a Bruin player was now open.

She spotted Collette Cunningham in front of the goal. Mia stutter-stepped and created a narrow gap between her two defenders. Before they could close in, she rocketed a cross pass to Cunningham.

Cunningham shot from twelve yards out, and the

ball found the left corner of the net. Now Lake Braddock led 2–0.

The goal broke Woodbridge's spirit. Mia later scored a second goal, and the Bruins went on to win, 4–1, to become state champions.

Mia didn't have much time to celebrate, however. The next day she and her two forward line teammates, Pike and Cunningham, played in a tournament game for the Shooting Stars. Each of the three Braddock High girls scored two goals as the team destroyed a Canadian team, 8–0. Team coach Denise Mishalow remarked after the game, "My job isn't too difficult. All I have to do is put them on the field and let them play."

A few weeks later, Mia graduated from high school. She rejoined the national team just in time to travel to Sardinia, Italy, where they played Poland to a 0–0 tie. Then it was time to prepare for college. Mia was on her way to Chapel Hill and the University of North Carolina.

Chapter Five:
1989–1990

National Champion

Mia was thrilled to be going to the University of North Carolina, but she was still like most teenagers who go away to college. She knew she would miss her family.

Her situation was made doubly difficult due to the fact that her father was again transferred, this time back to Italy. Although she had done a lot of traveling, she had never before been so isolated from her parents.

It helped that she already knew Coach Dorrance and many of her teammates, like her good friend Kristine Lilly, also a freshman at UNC. They soon became like a second family to her.

Still, Mia was under a lot of pressure at UNC. She became a political science major, and her academic program was tough and demanding. Even though

Mia was used to working hard at school, college-level work was much more difficult than her high school assignments had been.

Her commitments to the soccer team proved a challenge as well. College soccer season takes place in the fall, so as soon as school started, soccer season did, too. In addition to attending practices, all members of the team were expected to work out regularly with weights. They played a lot of games and did a lot of traveling.

Mia knew she was considered the team's most promising new recruit. The Tar Heels had gone undefeated since 1985 and had won three straight NCAA championships. She knew Coach Dorrance would be dissatisfied with anything less than another national title. Mia didn't want to let him or her new teammates down, but on a squad of so many good players, including two-time NCAA Player of the Year Shannon Higgins, Mia wasn't quite sure how she'd fit in. She knew the older girls on the team wouldn't have patience with what they referred to as "freshman mistakes."

She needn't have worried. While Mia later admitted that she felt insecure about her play that season, her performance spoke otherwise. She made the already powerful Tar Heel attack one of the most explosive in the history of collegiate women's soccer.

UNC plays in the tough Atlantic Coast Conference, or ACC. While they began the season ranked number one in the country, they played a tough schedule. Three other ACC teams, North Carolina State, Virginia, and Duke, were also ranked in the top twenty.

Still, the Tar Heels tore through the regular season, dispatching most opponents with ease. Higgins directed the attack from her position at midfield, and Mia teamed with fellow freshman Kristine Lilly to provide more than ample scoring punch from the forward line. This strong offense combined with a staunch, relentless pressure defense made the team a terror. On a tough late-season road trip, the longest in school history, the Tar Heels faced three top-twenty teams from the west coast — Santa Clara, St. Mary's, and Stanford — and defeated all three without allowing a single goal. Entering the ACC's post-season tournament, the team had racked up twelve consecutive wins while outscoring the opposition 77–6.

But the team knew they couldn't afford to take the tournament for granted. Despite winning the national title in 1988, they had lost the ACC championship in the season-ending tournament the previous season when, following a 1–1 tie to North Carolina State, UNC lost the league title on a penalty kick tiebreaker. While the standoff had preserved their unbeaten record, it had provided little satisfaction for the Tar Heels. NC State had all the bragging rights.

For the second consecutive year, they faced the Wolfpack of NC State in the finals of the ACC tournament. With a record of 21–0–1, the Tar Heels appeared to be a shoo-in over their cross-state rivals, who had compiled a record of 13–7–2. But Coach Dorrance thought otherwise.

Although he admitted that the 1989 Tar Heels were "the most exciting team we've ever had," Dorrance added a measure of caution to those who considered his team a dynasty.

The wins didn't come automatically. North Carolina still had to play. "We're only a dynasty in the sense that we've worked hard," he said. "We have strived for a goal and are reaching it."

When the Tar Heels met NC State, Mia Hamm took the biggest step toward reaching that goal by scoring some goals of her own. For the first time all year, the Tar Heel defense was surprisingly porous and allowed three goals. Fortunately, Mia and Kristine Lilly responded to the challenge. Each player tallied two goals as UNC dumped NC State, 5–3. Mia Hamm, a freshman and the youngest player on the field, was named the most valuable player of the tournament.

But the Tar Heels weren't quite finished with the ACC runner-ups. Both teams qualified for the NCAA tournament. After UNC blasted Hartford 9–0 in the quarterfinals, NC State was all that stood between the Tar Heels and another appearance in the finals. The semifinal matchup proved to be a repeat of the ACC championship game.

On a team of veterans, no one proved more adept at handling the pressure of the tournament than Mia Hamm. In the first half, with the game scoreless, she picked up a loose ball just outside the penalty area and blasted a shot past the goalie to put

UNC ahead, 1–0. Then, just ninety seconds into the second half, Kristine Lilly also scored. The Tar Heels shut down the Wolfpack to win, 2–0.

They faced Colorado College in the finals. Shannon Higgins demonstrated why she had once again been named Player of the Year. Incredibly, for the fourth year in a row, she scored the game-winning goal in the NCAA finals. The Tar Heels won, 2–0, capturing their fourth straight NCAA title.

While Higgins and Kristine Lilly garnered most of the headlines that season, Mia Hamm led the team in goals scored, with twenty-one. But she wasn't satisfied. She knew that most observers considered her primarily an offensive player whose all-around skills were just a notch below those of her more illustrious teammates. She vowed to make improvements in the off-season.

She continued to work hard on her conditioning. During training camp in the summer of 1990 with the national team, she peppered Coach Dorrance with questions about strategy and ways she could improve her game. She wanted to make certain the UNC dynasty continued.

As a result, her play improved. In their first game

of the summer, against Norway, one of the best teams in the world, Mia scored her first goal in international competition. The U.S. national team went on to have its most successful season to date, winning all six games they played. The icing on the cake came when FIFA announced that in 1991 they would sponsor the first women's World Cup tournament. Mia was thrilled.

Mia returned to Chapel Hill in the fall, ready for another winning season. But many observers thought the UNC women's soccer program had peaked. The loss of Shannon Higgins and several other experienced seniors left the Tar Heels with one of their youngest teams since the program had begun, in 1979. Mia had grown accustomed to being one of the youngest members of every team she had played for. Now, all of a sudden, she was a veteran. Her teammates looked to her to be a leader.

At the beginning of the 1990 season, the Tar Heels picked up right where they had left off the season before. But when they went on the road to face the University of Connecticut on September 22, the unthinkable happened. They lost in overtime, 3–2, ending the team's unbeaten streak at a remarkable 103.

After the game, the UConn players piled up on one another and hundreds of delirious fans raced onto the field. UNC left the field in an unfamiliar position, defeated.

Soccer fans all over the country were shocked, and some of Mia's own teammates were devastated. The team was accustomed to winning and dominating their opponents. In those 103 games, the Tar Heels had trailed for only 19 minutes and 45 seconds out of 9,270 minutes of play.

That may have been the reason they lost. When the team realized they couldn't shake the UConn team, some of Mia's teammates had panicked. Mia was one of the few players who had retained her composure, scoring both UNC goals. She realized it would be up to her to get the Tar Heels back on track.

But a week later, the team was still in trouble. Despite facing a young George Mason University team, which had won only twice all year, the powerful Tar Heels played poorly. It appeared as if the loss to

UConn had caused the team to begin to doubt itself. Perhaps the dynasty was over.

For eighty-nine minutes, the two teams played to a 0–0 tie. George Mason goalie Hollis Kosko, normally a defender, played the game of her life, making nineteen saves. UNC's best chance to score had come in the forty-eighth minute, when Mia's twenty-five-yard rocket had rattled off the crossbar.

Late in the game, many Tar Heel players became desperate, and they botched several chances to put the ball into the net. Then, with only fifteen seconds left in the game, Mia Hamm took over.

As a George Mason defender tried to control the ball at midfield and make a pass, Mia charged in and cut off the passing angle. The ball shot toward her, and she blocked it with her foot. Then she took off down the left wing as the partisan crowd at George Mason's home field stood and yelled.

As Mia approached the goal, Kosko came out to meet her. By rushing Mia, Kosko hoped to cut down the angle to the goal and force her into an early shot.

But Mia's experience proved critical. She slowed and waited as the goalie approached, biding her time. Finally, Mia faked a shot and Kosko was forced to commit, cutting to one side and blocking that side of the net.

That's all Mia needed. In a blur, she flicked the ball to the opposite side. Kosko dove for the ball, but the slow rolling shot just eluded her and found the back of the net. With only eight seconds remaining in the game, Mia's shot had won the game for UNC, 1–0.

Her teammates mobbed her. She had stayed calm when everyone else had panicked. While all Mia would say after the game about her winning shot was "I guessed right," her teammates and coach knew better. She had become a leader.

Even Mia understood that. "I think I have a different role than I did last year," she said later. "I'm one of the more experienced players on the field now."

Dorrance was effusive in his praise. "She has the best acceleration of any player that plays the game right now in the world. Once she gets shoulder to shoulder with you, unless you pull her jersey or foul her, she's going to go by you."

The last-second win sparked the team. They soon returned to their usual dominating style of play.

Only now they looked to Mia to lead them. In the ACC tournament finals, the number one Tar Heels faced number three Virginia. In the first half, a scoreless tie, the Cavaliers outshot the Tar Heels and controlled play.

This time, no one on the North Carolina team panicked. After all, they had a not-so-secret weapon, Mia Hamm.

Early in the second half, the ball rolled out of bounds on the Virginia end and North Carolina was awarded a corner kick. Mia placed the ball on the ground, took a few steps back, and looked toward the goal as her teammates jockeyed for position in front of the net.

She took a deep breath and stepped quickly toward the ball, kicking it so it spun sideways through the air and curved toward the goalmouth.

As the shot rocketed in front of the goal, players from both teams jumped and tried to head the ball. The goalie leaped into the air and waved her hands at the ball.

No one touched it. Like a hawk coming in for the kill, the ball swooped down and hooked into the far corner.

"Score!" UNC led, 1–0. Late in the game, another corner kick by Mia was headed into the goal by teammate Paige Coley. UNC held on for a 2–0 win.

After the game, Mia downplayed her shot. "All I'm trying to do is get it in the vicinity of the [penalty] box," she said. When pressed by a reporter to say more, a modest Mia deferred, saying, "There's nothing more to say about it."

In the NCAA tournament, UNC blasted through the competition and reached the finals easily. The finals were scheduled to be played at Fetzer Field, their home turf. Everyone on the team was delighted when the University of Connecticut also won their semifinal matchup. The two teams would meet in the finals.

This time, North Carolina was ready. With Mia drawing the attention of the defense, Kristine Lilly scored two first-half goals. The Tar Heels dominated the offense, outshooting the Huskies 14–4. Then they put the game away in the second half, scoring four more times and limiting Connecticut to only three shots. The Tar Heels won their fifth straight NCAA title, 6–0.

One UConn player called their play "the best performance of soccer I've seen in my college career."

Mia spelled out the Tar Heels approach to the game. "Coach told us to remember who we are and what it means to play for North Carolina," she said. "We wanted to bury them psychologically in the first fifteen minutes, and that's exactly what we did."

Although Mia was thrilled with the victory and had led the NCAA in scoring, with 24 goals and 19 assists, the end of the season was bittersweet. As she walked across the campus after the game, with the trees blazing in full fall color, she tried to soak it all in and enjoy the moment.

In only a few weeks, it would all be over. In order to continue to play for the national team and participate in the first women's World Cup, Mia Hamm had to quit school.

Chapter Six:
1991

The World Cup

The upcoming World Cup competition, hosted by China, promised to be unlike any kind of soccer the women on the American team had ever before experienced. For while the level of play for women's soccer in the United States was rapidly improving, it still lagged behind that of many other nations, whose women's programs predated that of the United States by as much as a decade or more. The six straight American wins in the summer of 1990 had come against teams that were not at full strength.

Many European countries had a strong system of club teams, which allowed women players to hone their skills against the best players in the country. Japan even had a professional women's league. Some nations paid their players sizable salaries, allowing them the luxury of playing soccer full-time. Although a few American women such as Michelle Akers played overseas, after an American woman soccer player graduated from college, there was no-place in the U.S. to play and no one to play against. The Americans were at a disadvantage.

If the U.S. team was to catch up, it had to do so quickly. The Americans had less than a year to come together as a team, qualify for the tournament, and, if they did, play well in the final round. Between mandatory practices, training camps, tournaments, and so-called "friendlies" (exhibition matches against teams from other nations in which the results don't count), striving to reach the World Cup left the players no time to do anything else, such as having a job or going to school.

In exchange for their commitment to the team, the players received only room and board and the satisfaction of knowing they were doing everything possible to win the Cup and promote the cause of women's soccer throughout the U.S. and the world. If they were fortunate enough to win, the United States Soccer Federation (USSF), the governing body that controls soccer in the United States,

53

promised the women a $50,000 award to be divided equally among the members of the team.

Their male counterparts on the men's U.S. national team had it much easier. They were paid a salary and received far more support from the USSF than the women's team did. For example, when the men traveled to a foreign country, they usually stayed in a nice hotel. The women, on the other hand, were often housed in barrack-like hostels or in private homes.

Yet despite the inequity, most members of the team willingly gave up their jobs, left their families, postponed having children, put off marrying, or, like Mia Hamm, quit school in order to follow their dreams.

Although Mia later called her decision to leave UNC "the hardest thing I've ever had to do," at the same time she was excited. For an entire year, playing soccer, the game she loved, would be her full-time occupation.

Her decision also involved a rather harsh self-assessment of her abilities. Mia knew that despite everything she had accomplished at UNC, she was still considered something of a one-dimensional

University of North Carolina Tar Heel Mia Hamm takes the ball downfield.

Tony Quinn

Mia Hamm and other members of the national team before playing Finland on April 30, 1995. Mia is number nine. Veteran Michelle Akers is number ten, and emerging star Julie Foudy is number eleven.

Even Mia Hamm looks surprised after scoring a goal in the Americans' 6–0 win over Finland in a "friendly" played in Davidson, North Carolina, on April 30, 1995.

AP/Wide World Photos

Mia Hamm controls the ball early in the gold medal game at the Summer Olympics in Atlanta on August 1, 1996.

Tony Quinn

While a frustrated Chinese player looks on, Mia Hamm leads her team to the gold medal.

Tony Quinn

Mia Hamm celebrates her goal against Italy in the Women's World Cup match on June 8, 1997, in Washington, D.C. The U.S. won, 2–0.

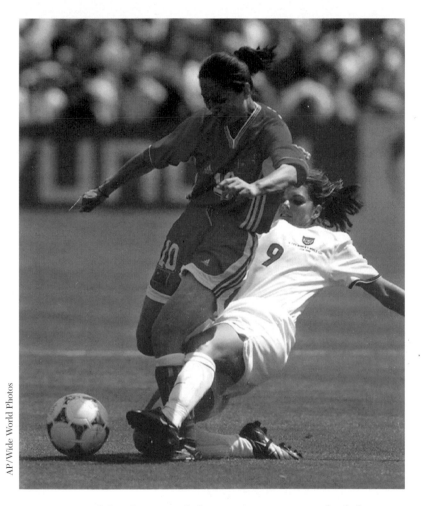

Mia Hamm slides for a steal during overtime period of the 1999 Women's World Cup final against China.

AP/Wide World Photos

Mia Hamm celebrates with her teammates after knocking in her penalty kick during the 1999 Women's World Cup final shootout.

Mia Hamm happily signs autograph after autograph for her fans.

Mia Hamm's Career Highlights

1987:
Member of the U.S. national team

1988:
Member of the U.S. national team

1989:
Member of the U.S. national team
Member of the NCAA women's soccer championship team
ACC tournament MVP

1990:
Member of the U.S. national team
Member of the NCAA women's soccer championship team
ACC Player of the Year

1991:
Member of the Women's World Cup championship team

1992:
National Player of the Year
Member of the U.S. national team
Set NCAA single-season scoring record (32 goals, 33 assists
  for 97 points)
Member of the NCAA women's soccer championship team
ACC Player of the Year
ACC tournament MVP

1993:
National Player of the Year
Member of the U.S. national team
Member of the NCAA women's soccer championship team
ACC Player of the Year
Recipient of the Mary Garber Award (ACC Female Athlete
  of the Year)

1994:

National Player of the Year

Member of the U.S. national team

Recipient of the Honda Broderick Cup (Most Outstanding Female Athlete in all college sports)

Recipient of the Mary Garber Award (ACC Female Athlete of the Year)

Named U.S. Soccer's Female Athlete of the Year

1995:

MVP of the U.S. Cup

Led U.S. national team in scoring (19 goals, 18 assists for 56 points in 21 games)

Named U.S. Soccer's Female Athlete of the Year

1996:

Olympic gold medalist

Led U.S. national team in scoring (9 goals, 18 assists for 36 points in 23 games)

Appeared in her 100th international match on January 18, vs. Ukraine

Named U.S. Soccer's Female Athlete of the Year

1997:

Named Women's Sports Foundation Athlete of the Year

Named U.S. Soccer's Female Athlete of the Year

MVP of Guangzhou International Tournament

1998:

Member of Goodwill Games gold medal team

Scored her 100th goal, the third player in women's soccer to do so

Named U.S. Soccer's Female Athlete of the Year

1999:

Member of the Women's World Cup championship team

Scored her 108th goal to become the world's highest scoring female player

Mia Hamm's College Stats

Year	Games Played	Games Started	Goals	Assists	Points
1989	23	18	21	4	46
1990	22	22	24	19	67
1992	25	21	32	33	97
1993	22	22	26	16	68
TOTALS	92	83	103	72	278

Mia Hamm's National Team Stats

Year	Games Played	Games Started	Goals	Assists	Points
1987	7	4	0	0	0
1988	8	7	0	0	0
1989	1	0	0	0	0
1990	5	1	4	1	9
1991	28	24	10	4	24
1992	2	2	1	0	2
1993	16	16	10	4	24
1994	9	9	10	5	25
1995	21	20	19	18	56
1996	23	23	9	18	36
1997	16	16	18	6	42
1998	21	21	20	20	60
TOTALS	157	143	101	76	278

Mia Hamm's Olympic Stats

Year	Games Played	Games Started	Goals	Assists	Points
1996	4	4	1	3	5

player, someone who was a constant threat to score goals but lacked the all-around game of players such as Tar Heel teammate Kristine Lilly. Mia felt that for the rest of her game to develop, it was best if she left UNC, where she would undoubtedly remain the focal point of the Tar Heel offense. On the national team, she'd be forced to develop all her skills. Lilly, on the other hand, already played a complete game and chose to stay at UNC.

The team of sixteen players and several alternates first got together in January for five days of intensive training, followed by a similar camp in February. In late March, they came together once more to prepare for a tournament in Bulgaria. For the next nine months, they spent virtually every moment together.

The intense schedule actually worked to the team's advantage. Many European teams didn't start playing together full-time until club leagues ended in the spring. No matter how talented they were as individuals, it still took time to learn to play together.

The Americans, on the other hand, bonded quickly. Nearly half the team had once played for Dorrance at North Carolina, so they were already familiar with his system and with one another.

That still didn't mean it would be easy. Because of injuries to other players, Mia had to adapt to a different position on the national team. She had always played forward in high school and college, but on the national team she played right midfielder, a position with greater defensive responsibilities. On offense, her primary duty was to be a playmaker, feeding the ball to her team's forwards. While she would still have opportunities to score goals herself, they would have to come within the team's offensive concept.

The change had the exact effect Mia had hoped for when she joined the team. It forced her to elevate her game and use a wider variety of skills than she was accustomed to.

For the first time in her life, Mia actually had to battle for a place on the team. Dorrance wasn't reserving a spot on the team for anyone. If a player didn't produce, there were several alternates willing to take her place.

The team played well together in Bulgaria and gained confidence, winning five matches in seven days, all shutouts, against teams from the host country, the USSR, Yugoslavia, Hungary, and France. As soon as they returned to the United States, they were off once more, this time to Haiti, where they had to play a round-robin tournament against other North American and Caribbean countries in order to qualify for the final round of sixteen teams.

They won all five games with ease, shutting out all five opponents and scoring an amazing 47 goals.

The team followed by touring Europe in May and playing five friendlies, against France, England, Holland, Denmark, and Germany. They won only three of five games.

The losses alarmed everyone on the team. They knew they would have to play much better to have a chance to win the Cup.

The team spent most of June and July in training camp before traveling to China for a series of three friendlies against the Chinese. They returned to the United States with only a single victory.

Things didn't get much better when they played host to two pairs of friendlies against Norway and China in the United States. Both visiting teams were expected to do well in the finals. The U.S. lost twice to Norway and split with China. In their last twelve games against international competition, their record was a lackluster 5–6–1.

When the team traveled to China to begin the final round in mid-November, no one expected the United States to do very well. Yet despite its record, the U.S. team itself was cautiously optimistic.

The Americans' recent losses had given them a clear picture of where they needed to improve. They seemed to play better when they played aggressively, attacking the goal. When they stayed back and let the other team determine the pace of the game, they had trouble. With several key players nursing injuries, they hadn't been at full strength earlier in the fall. Now just about everyone was healthy.

Mia had adjusted well to midfield. She discovered that her acceleration, which had served her so well at forward, was equally useful in her new position. And at five foot four and 125 pounds, she was strong enough to mark other players. She found that she could track most of her opponents, and if they made a mistake and lost control of the ball, she could instantly turn to the offensive side of her game and force play downfield. It was a bonus that her North Carolina teammate Kristine Lilly had decided to take leave from school and rejoin the squad. She played opposite Mia at left midfield, and the two players knew they could depend on each other.

The team's offense focused on striker Michelle Akers, a member of the team since 1985 and widely considered one of the best players in the world. Strong and aggressive, the five-foot ten-inch Akers had the hardest shot in women's soccer. One male coach, a former professional goalie, said her shots were "like cannonballs when you catch them."

As the youngest player on the team, Mia admired her teammates, particularly Akers. "Usually she draws a crowd of defenders around her," said Hamm when asked to describe a typical Akers goal, "and when she gets the ball, she turns and gets hit, then she turns again and gets hit again, then she claws her way through the pack, calms herself, and strikes the ball perfectly. She's so composed and focused."

The Americans played their first World Cup game on November 17, 1991, against a tough Swedish team. They went into the game knowing that a single loss would probably be enough to prevent them from winning the championship.

After a hard-fought contest, the Americans won in a mild upset, 3–2. Then they defeated Brazil 5–0 two days later. They followed with two more wins, 3–0 against Japan and 7–0 against Taiwan in a game in which Akers scored an amazing five goals. When they gook the field against Germany on November 27, they were just one game away from reaching the finals.

Riding a wave of emotion, the Americans swamped the German team, 5–2. Their aggressive play had made the difference. With Mia and Kristine Lilly challenging every ball and forcing play back toward the German goal, the Germans simply couldn't catch up.

Meanwhile, the team from Norway cruised through the tournament and reached the finals easily. For the American team, years of hard work and sacrifice would come down to a single game.

No one expected the Americans to win. After all, just two months earlier, the Norwegians had twice beaten the U.S. squad on American soil.

When the American team took the field at Tianhe Stadium on the evening of November 30, they could hardly believe their eyes. Sixty-five thousand fans packed the stadium, and the Chinese crowd cheered the American squad like they'd never been cheered before. Chinese fans had enjoyed the Americans' style of play and, as the "Cinderella" team of the tournament, had adopted them as their own.

But the support of the crowd wouldn't be of much help once the game began. The Americans knew that in order to win, they had to play their best game ever.

At the opening whistle, the U.S. team tried to go on the attack. But the Norwegian squad knew what to expect. They turned the tables and went on the offensive themselves, keeping the ball in the American zone for most of the half.

But the U.S. team made the most of their few opportunities. Despite being double- and triple-teamed, Akers scored on a header to put the Americans ahead, 1–0. Norway quickly knotted the score. At halftime, the game was tied.

In the second half, Norway dominated the play.

The American squad could do little on offense. It seemed as if it was just a matter of time before Norway would score and win the game.

Yet the U.S. team held on. Mia Hamm raced all over the field, running down the ball and disrupting Norway's attempts to set up its offense. Even when Norway did penetrate far downfield, one American player after another made a spectacular play to keep the opponents from scoring.

As the end of the game approached, however, it became obvious that the Americans were running out of steam. The Norwegians played patiently and didn't panic. They appeared unconcerned about winning in regulation and seemed to be saving their strength for almost certain overtime.

The American team sensed that, and as the clock ticked down, everyone drew on their final reserve of energy. It was now or never for the American women's soccer team.

But the Norwegians continued to stall. Then, with three minutes left, they made a crucial error.

Deep in their own zone, they made a halfhearted effort to move downfield, then slowed as the Americans desperately chased after the ball. Playing it safe at the eighteen yard line, Tina Svensson of Norway decided to make a back pass to goalie Reiden Seth. Seth slowly jogged out to meet the pass.

Michelle Akers, drawing on years of experience, sensed what was about to happen. As Svennson turned and made a weak pass back, Akers charged, crashing by Svennson and knocking her into a second defender. Both Norwegians stumbled and fell as Akers chased down the ball.

The move shocked the Norwegian goalie, who found herself out of position ten yards from the goalmouth with Michelle Akers streaking past her on the left toward the goal. As she shot past, Seth screamed, but her call for help did no good.

Akers was all alone in front of the net. And as Mia Hamm had noted, Michelle Akers knew how to keep her composure. From six yards out, she calmly stroked the ball with her right foot into the untended net.

"GOAL!" Michelle's teammates swarmed over her in celebration, then quickly retreated. There was still three minutes left to play.

In desperation, Norway sent the ball downfield, but Mia and her teammates drew on their last reserves of energy and turned them back. Then, suddenly, a whistle blew.

The United States had won.

For a moment, no one on the team moved. They just looked at one another in a combination of disbelief and unbridled delight. Then they ran toward one another, laughing and crying and hugging. A few players fell to the ground sobbing with joy. The normally placid Anson Dorrance raced from the American bench and joined his team on the field.

The Chinese crowd cheered wildly as the bitterly disappointed Norwegian team offered feeble congratulations and made way for the champions of the world. A podium was pulled onto the field, and each player received a gold medal and a huge bouquet of flowers. Coach Dorrance was presented with an enormous gold trophy signifying the win as the Chinese shot fireworks into the air.

In an interview, midfielder Julie Foudy spoke for Mia and all their teammates: "When we started the team, we never thought there would be a World Cup. It was always a mystical thing. And now we're holding it."

They had done it.

Chapter Seven:
1992–1993

Back to School

Despite its drama, the American women's victory in the first women's World Cup caused barely a ripple back in the United States. As far as the media was concerned, on a scale of relative importance, women's soccer ranked somewhere below professional wrestling. Most newspapers didn't even report the win at all. The few that did so carried little more than the score.

Yet for the members of the team, the championship meant everything in the world. Even if few others recognized their achievement, they knew what they had accomplished together. Never before had an American soccer team, male or female, won a world championship. For the American women to do so in the first women's competition even held was extraordinary, the culmination of years of sacrifice and hard work. But now that the competition was over and the next World Cup not scheduled until 1995, it was time to go back to the real world.

For some members of the team, their lives as soccer players were over. They had to find jobs and resume living a normal life. For others, it meant trying to find something to do until the national team reformed in the summer of 1992. For Mia Hamm, it was time to go back to school.

Despite the absence of both Mia and Coach Dorrance, UNC had still managed to win yet another ACC and NCAA title in 1991. Kristine Lilly won the Player of the Year Award.

Mia relished the opportunity to return to Chapel Hill. Her time with the national team had been hard work. She looked forward to relaxing for a while and living life as a normal college student. She and several teammates shared an off-campus apartment. The group of women had a great time living together and grew close.

When the Tar Heels began practice in the fall of 1992 for the upcoming season, it became obvious to everyone that Mia Hamm was a different player. During her year with the national team, Mia had improved dramatically, shedding the perception that she was a one-dimensional player. In fact, the World Cup official report had even cited her for being one of the best attacking defenders in the tournament. Even Mia admitted that she now had "a much better understanding of what it takes to be a playmaker." When she rejoined the Tar Heels on the field, she demonstrated just how much she had learned.

Installed on the forward line with Lilly, Mia Hamm had one of the most remarkable seasons of any collegiate athlete, male or female, in any sport, ever. She dominated play as no female soccer player had ever done before.

Her performance against Duke in the ACC finals epitomized her season.

Entering the game, UNC's record was 22–0. Mia led the nation in both goals and assists. But Duke was almost as good. They had lost only four games all year long.

In the first half, Mia helped UNC break through. A little more than sixteen minutes into the match, she penetrated to the edge of the penalty area just to the right of the goal.

In previous seasons, Mia would have tried to take her defender one-one-one, a strategy that might have resulted in a goal but was more likely to end with the ball either being deflected out of bounds or in Duke's possession. But now Mia drew on her experience on the national team. She hesitated for a moment, drawing the attention of the defense, then spotted Lilly open on the left side. She hit her with a flawless pass, and Lilly knocked the goal home. UNC led, 1–0.

But just moments into the second half, Duke scored and tied the score. It was only the second time all season that UNC hadn't led in the second half.

Mia's teammates turned to her. As she said later, "The last emotion you want to display to your teammates is one of disappointment. It was my job to motivate the other players. There was still a lot of time left."

Mia didn't panic. UNC needed to score. Instead of waiting for the game to come to her, Mia went out and took it. She expanded her game and made use of her speed to hound Duke on the defensive end. With only fifteen minutes remaining, she won a ball and hit Lilly with another spectacular pass. Lilly re-layed the ball to teammate Rita Tower for a goal to put UNC ahead, 2–1.

UNC could have played defensively, trying to protect the lead, but Mia was on fire. A few minutes later, she spotted Danielle Egan wide open in the penalty area. From an amazing forty-five yards away, Mia booted yet another perfect pass. Egan headed the ball in, and UNC's 3–1 victory, and another ACC championship, was assured.

Mia hadn't scored a goal, but she had collected three assists and dominated play for all ninety minutes. After the game, Duke coach Bill Hempen was in awe of Mia. "She's probably the best women's soccer player in the world," he said. "She showed that today." That may have been the first time anyone had ever said Mia was the best in the world. But it wouldn't be the last.

One month later, in the NCAA finals, Mia had the chance to demonstrate her skills to Duke once more. Duke fought its way to the finals, as did UNC. The Duke Blue Devils, who had been hoping for a rematch, got their wish.

This time, the two teams met on Fetzer Field, the

Tar Heels' home turf. Yet the Blue Devils refused to be intimidated. They played tough and, seventeen minutes into the game, scored on a header off a corner kick to take a 1–0 lead.

Now UNC trailed for the second time all year. Yet once again, Mia Hamm didn't panic. Ten minutes later, at the twenty-eight-minute mark, she took over the game again. Over the next few moments, her performance keyed perhaps the best stretch of soccer any Tar Heel team had ever played.

First Mia slipped in a shot from twelve yards out into the right corner of the net to tie the score. Then, five minutes later, as the Duke defense was distracted by Mia and Lilly, Keri Sanchez slipped in a goal on a corner kick to put UNC ahead, 2–1.

Twenty-four seconds later, Mia intercepted a sloppy pass and banged in another goal on a breakaway. Four minutes later, UNC scored again.

All of a sudden, the Tar Heels led 4–1. Duke was reeling.

The second half was all North Carolina. Coach Dorrance even took Mia out of the game, but the Tar Heels still kept scoring.

With eighteen minutes remaining, and the Tar Heels up 7–1, Mia pestered Dorrance into putting her back into the game. She wanted to play the final minutes with senior Kristine Lilly, who was playing her last game for the Tar Heels.

"We don't enjoy embarrassing teams," he explained later, "but there's no way I would prevent Mia from playing with the person she admires most."

Mia celebrated with her third and final goal of the match, and UNC won, 9–1, finishing the season a perfect 25–0 and capturing their seventh consecutive NCAA title. For the season, North Carolina outscored the opposition an amazing 132–11.

Coach Hempen struggled to find the right words: "They're just awesome, outstanding, unbelievable, anything you can say." Most observers felt that the 1992 Tar Heels represented the greatest collegiate women's soccer team ever.

At the end of the season, Mia won just about every women's soccer award imaginable, ranging from a unanimous selection as U.S. Soccer Female Athlete of the Year to being named the MVP of both the ACC and NCAA tournaments. She had led the nation in scoring, with a record 92 points and 33 assists.

That winter, she spent a few weeks in training with the national team. Then in March she accompanied the team to Cyprus for a three-game series against Denmark, Norway, and Germany.

The team learned that as defending World Cup champions, they were now targeted by every opponent. There would be no such thing as an easy match. A win against the Americans could make a team's season.

Sure enough, after defeating Denmark 2–0, the Americans lost to both Norway and Germany, 1–0.

The American victory in the World Cup had served as a wake-up call to women's soccer teams from other nations. Before the Cup, they had assumed that they were better than the United States. But the American win had exposed weaknesses in their soccer programs. They were working hard to catch up.

They proved precisely how hard they were working in the summer of 1993. The U.S. team entered the World University Games as heavy favorites. But after reaching the finals with little difficulty, they lost to China. With the next World Cup only two years off, the American women knew that in order to repeat their number one spot, they would have to play a lot better.

Yet as fall approached, the only goal that concerned Mia Hamm was for North Carolina to repeat as ACC and NCAA champions. Despite all the Tar Heels had achieved during her career, she wanted to make sure there was no letdown her senior season.

While the 1993 Tar Heels weren't quite as potent as they had been the year before, they were no less effective. Once again, they charged through the regular season with an unblemished record. Even though Mia was now usually double- or triple-teamed, her playmaking ability made it possible for some of her teammates, such as sophomore scoring sensation Tisha Venturini, to pick up the slack.

Yet Mia remained the player UNC looked to when things got desperate. Late in the season, always-tough Duke held Mia scoreless in the first half and looked capable of upsetting the top-ranked Tar Heels. But in the second half, Mia got going.

After just a few minutes of play, she streaked

down the field on the right side and found herself covered by only a single defender. Her opponent had little chance. Mia stutter-stepped around her as if the woman were standing still, then drilled the ball into the narrow gap between the diving goalie and right goalpost.

A few minutes later, she was at it again, this time fighting her way to reach a corner kick, which she expertly headed into the net. By the time she scored her third goal of the half a few minutes later, another UNC win and ACC championship were assured.

But perhaps the most memorable moment of that season took place off the field. Mia and several of her teammates were sitting around their apartment, which some referred to as "Animal House" due to its constant state of disarray. They were all watching a soccer game, when the phone rang. One of the women answered it, listened for a moment, then just started screaming.

One more dream seemed about to be fulfilled. They learned that women's soccer had just been added to the summer Olympic Games as a full medal sport, scheduled to be held in Atlanta in 1996!

Mia couldn't believe it. "I grew up on the Olympics," she remembered later. "I distinctly remember 1984, cheering all the greats on like Mary Lou Retton and Jackie Joyner-Kersee. My heroes and idols.

"Here I was, playing a sport and participating in an Olympic development program, and we weren't even an Olympic sport. For me, the Olympics was always the next step.

"What an incredible opportunity. You hear all the clichés, that it's a dream come true. Well, it is, for myself and for every young girl growing up who plays any sport."

But before that dream could come true, Mia still had to complete her final collegiate season at UNC. Looking for their eighth straight NCAA title, the Tar Heels met George Mason in the finals at Fetzer Field. Nearly six thousand fans, a record number to see a collegiate women's soccer match, turned out for the game. Most were there to see Mia Hamm play her final collegiate game.

Mia's teammates were determined to win. They didn't take any chances.

Only two minutes into the game, Keri Sanchez scored on an unassisted goal to put UNC ahead, 1–0. Then the Tar Heel defense went to work.

They shut George Mason down, not allowing them a single shot on goal during the entire first half. Meanwhile, UNC scored twice more, including one goal assisted by Mia.

In the second half, with UNC ahead 3–0, Mia broke to the ball and won it from a George Mason defender. Then she shot past, dribbling the ball and streaking toward the net.

The George Mason goalie didn't have a chance. Mia drilled the shot to put UNC ahead 4–0. It was the last goal of her collegiate career.

Late in the game, with victory assured, Coach Dorrance pulled Mia from the game. Action stopped as her teammates surrounded her, tears in their eyes, and all 5,721 fans stood and cheered for Mia, making as much noise as a crowd two or three times that size. After the final whistle of the 6–0 UNC win, no one really wanted to talk about how it was North

Carolina's eighth straight championship. They just wanted to talk about Mia.

"There will never be a player who will break Mia's records," said Coach Dorrance of her NCAA career record 278 career points. "They're secure until the end of time. She came here during an incredible era of striking and scoring power."

True to form, Mia didn't have much to say about her accomplishments. She gave credit to her teammates. "The records are not important," she said after the game. "What it shows is the strength of the program and the traditions of the school. It's reflective of the people I'm surrounded with.

"The goals and the championships are nice, but the emotions, the tears, and the smiles on my teammates' faces are my championships."

She didn't know it then, but in the next few years, there would be both smiles and tears for Mia Hamm.

Chapter Eight:
1994–1995

Disappointment

At the end of the season, Mia collected virtually every award and accolade possible. Not only did she repeat as national and ACC Player of the Year, but she was also named the Mary Garber Award winner as ACC female Athlete of the Year and was the recipient of the Honda Broderick Cup, given to the most outstanding female athlete in collegiate sports.

The awards were nice, but after graduating from college, Mia was already looking ahead. In the summer of 1994, while the men's World Cup was being staged in the United States for the first time, the women's national team would again have to qualify for the women's World Cup. If they did, they then would get a chance to repeat their title in Sweden in 1995. After that, Mia hoped to compete in the Olympics.

The hype that surrounded the 1994 men's World Cup raised the profile of soccer in the United States. That event, coupled with the addition of women's soccer as an Olympic medal event, dramatically changed women's soccer. The national team, which had thus far played and practiced in obscurity, was suddenly the focus of much more attention. Magazines profiled the team's best players. Corporations realized that the U.S. squad would be favored to win a medal in Atlanta. All of a sudden, they were interested in helping to sponsor the national team.

Almost overnight, the women's team began to be treated almost as well as the men's team. Plans were made to create a training center for the team in Florida, and team members were put on salary, which allowed them to focus entirely upon the World Cup. Mia even signed an endorsement contract with Nike, the sporting goods company. It was an exciting time to be a female soccer player.

But other nations had the same reaction to the news about the Olympics. They, too, started paying more attention to the sport. Women's professional leagues had sprouted up in Sweden, Norway, and Germany. The upcoming women's World Cup promised to be much more competitive. The American team wouldn't have an easy time repeating as champions. As Mia commented to a reporter, "Any one of the teams could beat us this year. We're all basically equal in talent."

In 1994, Coach Dorrance shocked everyone when he announced that he was stepping down as head coach of the national team. Collegiate soccer was expanding rapidly, and he felt he could no longer serve as coach of both the national team and UNC. It would be up to new coach Tony DiCicco to get the team together.

The American team had little difficulty in the qualifying round, defeating all four opponents while giving up only a single goal. Mia played extremely well. Against the team from Trinidad and Tobago, she nailed four goals in an 11–1 win.

Yet everything wasn't perfect for the Americans. Michelle Akers was ill with chronic fatigue syndrome, and no one was certain how much she would be able to play in the World Cup or even if she was going to play at all. There were several new members of the team, too, which meant adjustments for everyone, including Mia.

At the same time, Mia's personal life changed. After having dated for several years, she and Christian Corey, a Marine pilot, were married on December 17, 1994.

In the year leading up to the World Cup, the team appeared to be just as strong as they had been in 1991. In fourteen friendlies played between the qualifier and the Cup finals, the team lost only once, to Denmark, and tied Norway. When the final round began, in June 1995, the U.S. team had won its last nine matches.

Mia was back playing right forward and appeared right at home. As the team prepared for the Cup, she led the squad by scoring twelve goals in fourteen games. Now, just about everyone recognized her as perhaps the greatest player in the game. Teammate Carin Gabrerra, at age thirty a team veteran, commented that "we've watched her mature into one of the best players in the world." That kind of talk made Mia self-conscious and a little embarrassed. When someone would ask her if she was the best player in the world, she usually just shook her head and laughed, saying, "I'm not even close." She didn't even think she was the best player on her team.

Yet she was, by far, the team's most versatile player. Over the past several years, she had improved every aspect of her game. As she said later, "I worked really hard on my fitness, and I worked really hard on my defensive presence, and what I learned was that I was a lot more confident offensively because of that. I was never tired. A lot of my offensive confidence came from defensive success, winning the ball from a defender and then going forward. I wasn't just thinking, 'Geez, Mia, don't mess up.'" In an emergency, she was even listed as the team's third-string goalkeeper. Coach DiCicco said, "When Mia is on, there's no one better in the world."

But during the World Cup, Mia wasn't on, and neither was the rest of the team. In the opening match of the tournament, on June 6, the U.S. received a shock. They were tied by China, 3–3. It had been three years since the U.S. team had given up so many goals in a game.

The tie put the squad in a tough spot. Teams in the finals were divided into groups. In order to reach the finals, a team had to finish either first or second in the group. One more loss could prevent the U.S. from even reaching the final round.

In their second game, the U.S. rebounded to take a 2–0 lead against Denmark. But with only six minutes remaining in the game, goalkeeper Briana Scurry was ejected on a controversial hand-ball infraction outside the goal box. Since the United States had already used up its allotment of three substitutions, Mia Hamm had to step into the goal while the U.S. played shorthanded.

The Danes sensed an opportunity. Apart from winning the Cup outright, defeating the defending champs and knocking them from the finals would be the next best thing.

They swarmed the American end and, moments after Mia went into goal, were awarded a free kick. Mia hardly knew what to do.

Her teammates formed a wall between the shooter and the goal. Mia danced back and forth as various teammates told her where to line up. She was still jockeying for position when the Dane took a shot. Fortunately for Mia, it soared over the net.

But her ordeal wasn't over. In the final seconds of

the game, a Danish player worked free and took a hard shot. This time Mia was in position. She caught the ball against her stomach, and a few moments later, the U.S. escaped with a 2–0 win.

After the game Mia admitted her stint as goalie left her "scared to death."

"The goal is so much bigger when you're inside it than when you're shooting at it," she said. "I hope I never have to do it again!"

She didn't. A few days later, the team dispatched Australia 4–1 to win their group, beating out China on a tiebreaker determined by the total number of goals scored.

Thus far, Mia had played steady but not spectacular soccer. Her former teammates at UNC, Lilly and Tisha Venturini, had taken up much of the scoring slack caused by Michelle Akers's absence. Defenses focused on Mia, so she found herself back in the role of playmaker. She drew the attention of the defense, then passed off to her teammates.

Led by Kristine Lilly's two goals, the U.S. team defeated Japan 4–0 in the quarterfinals to reach the semifinals. The win was a big one for the United States. Coach DiCicco had gambled and chosen to rest Michelle Akers, who was still weak and had also suffered a concussion and a knee injury the previous week. In the second half, with the U.S. leading 3–0, he had rested several other players, including Mia Hamm. He wanted the team at full strength for their semifinal matchup against Norway.

Since the 1991 Cup finals, the American and Norwegian women's soccer teams had become arch rivals. The U.S. had faced Norway more than any other team in the world, except Canada. Many observers believed they were the two best teams in the world.

But in six meetings since the 1991 Cup final, the U.S. had won only once. Norway played the Americans tough. Before the game, Coach DiCicco admitted, "It will be a war. Their players don't like our players. Maybe they're jealous — who knows?" Still, the United States was favored to win.

When the game began, the Americans knew immediately that they had to play extremely well in order to win. The Norwegians played a rough, physical game. From the opening minute, they had the Americans on the defensive.

Only ten minutes into the game, Norway scored

off a corner kick when a header bounced off the crossbar and into the goal. For the rest of the first half, the U.S. scrambled as Norway kept the pressure on.

In the second half, the Americans played better but just couldn't put the ball into the net. Michelle Akers was playing hurt and got off only one shot the entire game. Although the U.S. had several good scoring opportunities, they failed to make them work. Norway's single goal held up, and the U.S. lost, 1–0. The Americans were world champions no more.

This time, their tears were not of joy but of sadness, and it was the Americans who offered congratulations to the exuberant Norwegians. Michelle Akers summed up her teammates' feelings after the game when she said, "It's like having your guts kicked out of you." Added midfielder Julie Foudy, "It's like someone snatched away our dream."

A few days later, Norway easily defeated Germany to win the World Cup. The U.S. regrouped and shut out China 2–0 to finish third. In the Olympics, third place means a bronze medal.

Mia and her teammates wanted to wear gold.

Chapter Nine:
1996

The Olympic Team

"A lot of times, when I think about doing this," said Mia after the World Cup, "I think to myself, 'Man, I'm really tired.' I've been with this team for eight years. That's a career for a professional football player or basketball player."

Perhaps she had been tired during the World Cup. But if she was, the loss to Norway served to energize her. Just a few weeks after the World Cup, Mia couldn't wait to get back together with the team. She had something to prove.

As Mia explained later, when the team regrouped in Orlando in January of 1996, "We had kind of decided there were certain things we weren't going to do the same way, and there were certain things we were going to do better. Everyone committed themselves to doing that, to being fitter, to being faster, to being stronger, and bringing the team closer together, on the field and off."

The entire team lived together, practiced together, trained together, and even went out together at night. Orlando residents grew accustomed to seeing a large group of extremely fit women making occasional appearances in the city's nightspots.

The team members grew closer than ever before. They were dedicated to one goal, and one goal only: an Olympic gold medal. No one would be satisfied with anything less.

Mia set the tone for the entire team. As she told one interviewer, "I've worked too hard and too long to let anything stand in the way of my goals. I will not let my team down and I will not let myself down. I'm going to break myself in half to make sure it happens."

"It," of course, was winning a gold medal. "It's in the ninetieth minute that the gold medal will be won," she added, "when we all decide what our comfortable zone is and what our regular role on the team is and push ourselves beyond what we thought we could do. That's what it will take to win the gold."

But the road to the Olympics was long. For the American team, it began in Brazil.

After a short training period, in late January they traveled to Brazil and played four friendlies, winning three times and tying once. They used the series as a tune-up for a more important challenge just ahead. When they returned to Florida, they had to prepare for a two-game rematch with Norway.

Even though no title or championship was at stake, the American women always took Norway seriously. They knew they would probably have to face the Norwegians in the Olympics, and they needed a win to build their confidence.

In the first game, on February 2, Mia put the United States ahead with a first-half goal, and the team held on for a 3–2 win. But in the second game, two days later, with the game tied and only seconds remaining, Norway scored to win 2–1. The Americans would have to wait until the Olympics to get another chance at their biggest adversary.

The team used the defeat as extra motivation as they played host to a number of teams in a series of friendlies. Each time they played, they continued to improve.

But in March, the team barely avoided disaster. Late in a game against Germany, with the U.S. ahead 1–0, Mia pursued a pass over her head into the German goalkeeper's box. She was running full speed and collided with the goalie as she slid out to gather the ball.

Mia fell to the ground and lay motionless while her teammates gathered around her. She was just stunned but was unable to stand up. She left the field on a stretcher.

The U.S. team won the game, 2–0, but no one on the team really cared. They were just worried about Mia.

The team doctor diagnosed the injury as a sprained knee. Fortunately, after a few weeks of rest Mia would be okay.

Shortly after she returned, she played one of the most amazing games of her career. In a driving rainstorm in Indianapolis, she showed the team from France that she really was the best player in the world.

For twenty-three minutes, neither team could score as the sodden field held everyone in check.

But at the twenty-three-minute mark, Tisha Venturini found Mia ten feet from the French goal. She made an accurate pass, and Mia rocketed the ball into the net to put America ahead, 1–0.

Five minutes later, Mia launched another missile at the French goal. The goalkeeper managed to deflect it, but one of Mia's teammates knocked it home to give the U.S. a 2–0 lead.

One minute later, it was 3–0 after Mia tracked down a loose ball and put it past the French goalie. The U.S. scored again to go up 4–0, then Mia made yet another goal. Two minutes after that, she assisted on a goal by Michelle Akers, increasing the Americans' lead to 6–0. In the second half, she scored once more. In the 8–2 U.S. win, Mia scored four goals and assisted on two others. It was one of the greatest performances in the history of women's soccer.

By the time the Olympics began in late July, the U.S. women's soccer team was on a roll. They hadn't lost a game since the defeat by Norway five months earlier.

Much like the World Cup, the Olympic soccer

competition divided the women's teams into groups. To make it to the medal round, the Americans first had to make it through group play.

They played their first match on July 21 against Denmark. Although the Olympics were based in Atlanta, Georgia, Olympic soccer games were held in several different locations. The first game was played in Orlando, Florida, where the Americans trained.

Twenty-five thousand fans — at the time, the most ever to watch a women's soccer game in the United States — turned out for the first match under a grueling Florida sun. The temperature on the field was more than 100 degrees. Yet Mia Hamm sent everyone home happy. Everyone except the Danes, that is.

She was all over the field, hounding the ball on defense and leading the American attack. While everyone else was gasping for air, Mia ran around as if she had extra oxygen.

With the U.S. ahead 1–0, Mia took a header from Akers and put on a patented burst of speed that left her defender in desperate pursuit. Then, while running full speed, she blasted in a spectacular goal into the left corner from twelve yards out. It all happened so fast, most of the people in the crowd missed it.

Then, only four minutes into the second half, she did it again. She got the ball on the right side of the penalty area but found her path to the goal blocked by two defenders. She faked right, left, forward, and back, as the two Danish women stumbled and twisted to keep up. Then she burst by them and shuffled a short pass to teammate Tiffeny Milbrett, who kicked it into the net. The U.S. won, 3–0.

Mia's performance stunned soccer fans and media from around the world. They were accustomed to seeing such play in men's soccer, from players like the great Pelé or Argentine star Diego Maradona. But they were shocked to discover that a woman could play with the same combination of speed, strength, and grace.

"Every time she got the ball she was dangerous," explained Coach DiCicco after the game. "She was the key player for us. Mia took the game over."

Danish coach Keld Gantzhorn concurred. "We made a little mistake, and she said, 'Thank you' and scored. I am sure we saw one of the best teams in "competition," he added. "I am sure they will reach the final."

At the end of the day, that seemed even more likely. Heavily favored Norway was stunned by Brazil, and tied at 2–2. The Americans had the edge.

But the next game, two days later, demonstrated just how difficult it is to win an Olympic medal. The Swedish knew all about Mia's performance against Denmark, and they were determined not to let her beat them. She was double-teamed most of the match and marked closely. On at least seven different occasions she was knocked to the ground. The final time, following a collision with the Swedish goalkeeper, Mia crawled from the field on her hands and knees with a badly sprained left ankle.

Although the U.S. defeated Sweden 2–1, the player the team could least afford to lose was hurt. There was little time to recover. Coach DiCicco announced that Mia's playing status was "day-to-day."

They traveled to Miami to face China, always a tough team, on July 25. With either a win or tie, each team could qualify for the medal round.

After appearing in more than one hundred consecutive international matches for the American team, Mia couldn't play. Her ankle was so sore, she could barely walk.

Her teammates didn't let her down. With Mia out of the lineup, China decided to play a conservative, defensive game. The Americans dominated play and outshot China by more than a two-to-one margin, but couldn't score.

Neither could the Chinese. Both teams advanced in competition.

After their first-game tie with Brazil, Norway had recovered to win twice and also advance. The U.S. team had to face them in the semifinals on July 28. If the U.S. won, they would play the winner of the match between China and the surprisingly strong Brazilian team for the gold medal. If they lost . . . Well, no one on the team wanted to even think about losing.

Before the game, Mia had her ankle heavily taped. It was still sore and hurt to run on, but she felt she could play. Coach DiCicco put her back in the starting lineup. He knew that even if she wasn't quite at one hundred percent, Norway would still have to pay attention to her, and that might open up a goal-scoring opportunity for another player.

As always, the Norwegians played hard. They focused on defense and, taking a lesson from the Swedes, decided to play Mia close. Time after time she was sent tumbling to the ground. Her teammates' pleas for a penalty went unheeded.

Only eighteen minutes into the game, Norway took advantage of a rare lapse by the American defense. A Norwegian player got free on a breakaway and scored to put Norway ahead, 1–0.

The lead held through the first half. Although the Americans were dominating play, they just couldn't score.

Then with only twelve minutes to play, Mia got the ball in the penalty area. With the crowd roaring, several Norwegian players closed on her once more and knocked her viciously to the ground, stripping her of the ball. It looked as if the United States had just lost another scoring opportunity.

But this time the referee blew the whistle and stopped play. At long last, the official finally called a penalty on one of Mia's takedowns. The Americans would receive a penalty kick!

On another day, Coach DiCicco may have allowed Mia to take the kick herself. But he knew her ankle was sore, and besides, Michelle Akers still had the most powerful shot in all of women's soccer.

The ball was placed on the ground twelve yards from the goal. Players from both teams stood back and watched as Akers set up behind the ball. The Norwegian goalkeeper crouched, slowly rocking from one side to the other, trying to stay loose. The crowd hushed.

Then Akers took off toward the ball. The goalie dove, trying to anticipate her shot.

Boom! The kick ripped into the back of the net. "Goal!" The game was tied.

Twelve minutes later, it ended. But in the final round, there are no ties. The game entered overtime.

The U.S. team would not be denied the opportunity to play for the goal medal. Only ten minutes into overtime, midfielder Julie Foudy fed a pass to Shannon MacMillan, and on the American team's twenty-eighth shot of the game, the ball finally made it past the goalkeeper. The United States won, 2–1. Despite her sprained ankle, Mia Hamm had played every minute of the game.

Now it was time to go for the gold.

Chapter Ten:
1996

Golden Game

China easily defeated Brazil in the other semifinal to set up a rematch with the United States on August 1 for the gold medal. Although the Americans were heavy favorites, the team was determined not to take the Chinese team lightly.

"China is a very good team," warned Coach Di-Cicco. "In the group match, they played for a tie. We can't expect that in the final."

Nothing prepared the American team for the reception they received when they stepped out onto the field at Sanford Stadium. The huge arena was filled to capacity with more than seventy-six thousand fans, most of whom chanted, "USA! USA!" over and over.

Everyone on the team, including Mia Hamm, couldn't help but think back to the long practices and scrimmages they had played with no one watching at all, or the dozens of games they had played before only a few hundred fans. Their own effort and determination had helped turn women's soccer into a sport that people cared about. Each day, Mia received hundreds of fan letters from young soccer players. It was almost impossible for any of the women to walk around in public. Everywhere they went, they were mobbed by fans.

When Mia looked up into the crowd, she knew her parents, brother Garrett, and other brothers and sisters were all watching. She wanted to make them proud, particularly Garrett. His illness had slowly grown worse. He even had to quit his job to focus all his energies on his health. Although Mia had pulled a groin muscle in practice the previous day, adding to the discomfort already caused by her sore ankle, all that meant nothing compared to what he had been going through.

But as soon as Mia and her teammates started warming up, they forgot about the crowd. They were on the field for one reason and one reason only: to win the gold medal.

When the game began, the Americans soon learned

that Coach DiCicco had been right. The Chinese were playing much more aggressively. In the first few minutes of the game, most of the action took place at midfield as each team probed the other, looking for an opening.

Nineteen minutes into the game, Kristine Lilly carried the ball deep down the left flank. Without even thinking, Mia ran a parallel course down the right side. The two girls had played together for so long that each knew exactly what the other was going to do.

All of a sudden, Lilly sent a cross pass through the penalty area. As she did, Mia broke toward the ball, using her unmatched acceleration to reach it before the Chinese defenders knew what was happening.

Boom! She kicked the ball toward the goal, low to the ground.

The crowd started to roar, then stopped and began to groan as they saw the Chinese goalkeeper dive toward the ball and partially block it with her hand.

It careened to the side and thudded off the post.

Then they cheered again, louder and longer than any of the American women had ever heard a crowd cheer before. Because Shannon MacMillan, trailing the play, pounced on the rebound. She was accustomed to playing ricochets. In the off-season, she played for a men's indoor soccer team, where the ball remains in play after rebounding off walls. She deftly tapped the ball into the net. The U.S. led, 1–0.

But the Chinese didn't give up. They weathered another American attack a few minutes later, then slowly took control of play. At the twenty-nine-minute mark, with U.S. goalie Briana Scurry charging hard to meet her, Sun Wen of China lofted a soft shot just over Scurry's arms and into the net to tie the game. At halftime, the score was still 1–1.

As the Americans tried to catch their breath and Coach DiCicco moved from player to player offering words of encouragement, Mia was in a quandary. Her ankle throbbed, and she felt a sharp pain in her groin every time she ran at full speed. She was afraid she was hurting her team. Perhaps, she thought, it would be better if she sat out the second half.

She turned to teammate Shannon MacMillan and said, "I'm not able to run very well. Am I hurting the team? Should I take myself out?"

MacMillan looked at Mia as if she had just stepped off an alien spacecraft.

"Are you kidding?" she blurted out. "We need you. Even if you're not one hundred percent, the Chinese have to worry about you, which means someone else might get free."

Unconvinced, Mia asked several other teammates for their opinion. The vote was unanimous. Everyone thought Mia should keep playing.

In the second half, Shannon MacMillan's take on Mia's impact on the game proved to be accurate. Time after time, she led the American attack on the Chinese goal, only to be stopped by some brilliant work by the Chinese goalkeeper.

Then, with twenty-two minutes remaining, Mia got the ball again. She drove hard down the right side, and the Chinese defense came out to meet her.

As they did, she spotted teammate Joy Fawcett outrunning a defender. Mia hit her in stride with a perfect pass. Meanwhile, Tiffeny Milbrett had slipped past a defender in front of the net. Fawcett crossed the ball to Milbrett, who expertly kicked the ball past the Chinese goalie.

"Score!" Now the United States led, 2–1. A gold medal was only twenty-two minutes away.

For most of the American team, those twenty-two minutes seemed to take forever. China played as hard as they could, but the American defense just wouldn't break down.

Then, with only a minute left to play, Mia's ankle gave out. She fell to the ground. She had given everything she had and couldn't continue. As she had promised months before, she had pushed herself beyond what she thought she could do. She was carried from the field to the thunderous cheers of her fans.

Mia hadn't let her teammates down, and now they didn't let her down. Sixty seconds slowly ticked by as the U.S. team kept China at bay.

Then it was over. Mia Hamm and the United States women's soccer team had won!

From out of nowhere, flags were handed down from the stands and placed into the hands of the victorious American players, who ran around the field, waving to the cheering crowd.

As much as she wanted to, Mia couldn't join

them. She limped out to the middle of the field, a wide smile on her face. First supported on each side by two of the team's trainers, she was soon surrounded by her teammates after the victory lap for the gold medal ceremony. A band played "The Star-Spangled Banner," and as the American flag was raised, every member of the team looked up in tears at the crowd. It had taken a tremendous amount of work, but at that moment, no one on the team had any doubt that it had been worth it. For around each neck hung an Olympic gold medal.

After the game, the press crowded around Mia. They had correctly anointed her as the team's hero of the moment.

But as they pressed her to comment about her performance, Mia characteristically downplayed her own role and gave credit to her teammates. "This team is incredible," she told them. "We all believed in each other and we believed in this day. From the beginning, this has been an entire team effort."

It was up to Mia's teammates to speak up for her. "Mia impacts the game whether she scores or not," said Brandi Chastain. "She tears defenses apart. She is awesome."

Added Tisha Venturini, "Mia was incredible. I don't know how she kept going. She's something special."

On this day, millions of soccer fans all over the world agreed.

Chapter Eleven:
1996-1998

Moving Ahead

For Mia Hamm, the most gratifying moment of the Olympic Games came when the team returned to their hotel after the game. As Mia gingerly stepped from the van transporting the team, she spotted her brother Garrett.

Despite being seriously ill, he was not going to let anything prevent him from watching the game. He pushed through the crowd waiting to greet the team and put his arms around Mia. With tears streaming down his face, he whispered, "I'm so proud of you."

As Mia later admitted to a reporter, "That meant so much to me. It wouldn't have been complete without having Garrett there."

After that, the gold medalists did some serious celebrating. After all, they'd earned it.

Although Mia looked forward to taking a vacation

with her husband after the Olympics, she discovered she had precious little time to do so. After winning the gold medal, the women's team in general and Mia in particular were in demand. Almost overnight, Mia became a big star.

At least that's what others thought. As far as Mia was concerned, she was the same person she'd always been.

It seemed as if every magazine in the country wanted to interview her, and most asked the same question, "How does it feel to be the best women's soccer player in the world?"

Invariably Mia would just shake her head. "I'm not," she would insist over and over. Her protestations did little good. The American public had fallen in love with Mia Hamm.

Mia was in demand. Young girls considered her a hero, a notion Mia scoffed at. Yet she still felt responsible for setting a good example in life. When she made public appearances at soccer clinics or schools, she was invariably mobbed by groups of girls screaming her name and asking for her autograph. She signed as many as she could. She knew that for a young girl, meeting someone she considered a hero would make an impression. She wanted to make sure it was a positive one.

When she signed autographs and spoke before groups, she usually handed out a small flyer. It described the disease that afflicted her brother, aplastic anemia, and urged people to have a simple blood test done for bone marrow screening. Garrett and others with the disease needed a bone marrow transplant in order to survive. In Garrett's case, the situation was particularly dire. In most instances, family members can be donors, but since Garrett was adopted, no one in Mia's family was a match. If he didn't get a transplant soon, Garrett would die.

Mia's fame reached beyond young girls who played soccer. Corporate America discovered her and in the wake of the Olympics considered her to be the perfect spokeswoman. She did television and magazine endorsements for a variety of products, such as shampoo, sports equipment, soda, and nutritional sports bars.

After depending on her family for so long for financial support, Mia appreciated finally being able to support herself. But all the notoriety made her a little uncomfortable. "It's weird getting attention," she said. "I'm not this perfect person," she kept insisting.

She knew there was much more to life than winning gold medals and being famous. Garrett had taught her that. After waiting years for a transplant, in February 1997 an appropriate donor was finally located. Garrett underwent the operation.

At first, it appeared to be a success, as he began to feel like his old self. But he soon got sick again. He contracted a fungal infection. After being ill for so long, he was too weak to fight it off. In April, he died.

Mia was devastated. "I've been blessed by so many things," she said later, "but I would give them all up to have him back."

Mia knew that the last thing Garrett would have wanted was for her to stop reaching for her dreams. She was still a member of the national team and turned to her teammates for support. When they hosted the U.S. Women's Cup, every member of the team wore a black armband in Garrett's memory. The United States won the Cup, and Mia was named MVP.

But while her teammates helped Mia get through a difficult time, they also made certain that she didn't allow her sudden fame to go to her head. When *People* magazine selected her as one of the fifty most beautiful people in the world in May 1997, they teased her unmercifully.

Yet at the same time, they were also proud. As teammate Julie Foudy said, "Mia has natural beauty. It's not something she has to spend a thousand dollars on." They appreciated that the team was partly responsible for making people realize that it was okay for a woman to be an athlete and for helping young girls to see that it was to possible to play sports and still be considered a woman.

They needn't have worried about Mia getting a big head. No matter how much attention she got, she still considered herself a soccer player first. "If I had to give up what I'm doing," she said, "I wouldn't be happy."

Today, Mia's most important role remains as an ambassador for her sport and for women athletes in general.

"I've experienced every emotion on the field," she once said, "sadness, fear, and happiness." Soccer had made the difference in her life. "It made me who I am," she once confided to a reporter. "I was given a tremendous gift, and believe I was given it for a reason."

For millions of her fans, the reason has been the opportunity to watch her play. The gift she gives back is the proof that soccer is a game for everyone.

Chapter Twelve:
1997-1999

Taking Aim

1997 marked a year of possibilities for Mia. She had been named U.S. Soccer's Female Athlete of the Year for 1996, her third consecutive year, and now she was closing in on two important milestones: the 100 career goal mark and the world record for career goals.

But to Mia, reaching those personal goals took a backseat to helping the team be their best.

In October of 1997 in Chicago, the team learned that staying atop the world of women's soccer was going to be harder than they thought. Before an enthusiastic crowd of just over 7,000 fans, they lost to the Germans, 3–0, their first defeat in thirty-one matches.

The team was embarrassed by the defeat, but had

little time to dwell on the loss. Immediately after the game they flew to Germany for a rematch.

The confident Germans opened the game fired-up and in the first five minutes had two scoring chances. Then the Americans slowly took control.

In the thirty-first minute, Tiffeny Milbrett sent a delicate pass to Mia, who cut to the ball at the top of the penalty box. As the defender charged, Mia deftly sidestepped around her, took one step, and rolled the ball into the net with her left foot to put the U.S. ahead, 1–0.

Five minutes later Tisha Venturini scored to increase the lead to 2–0. And late in the game Mia added a second goal on a header off a long cross by Shannon MacMillan. The Americans won, 3–0.

But the Americans ended the 1997 season on a low note, losing to Brazil, 1–0. With the important Guangzhou Tournament in China on the horizon, the defending Olympic champions knew they had to start playing better.

That's just what they did. In China, they defeated Sweden and tied the host team to make it to the final against archrival Norway. They looked forward to meeting the Norwegians on the field. They hadn't forgotten how they felt when they lost the World Cup in 1995.

With the U.S. ahead, 1–0, Mia broke free late in the first half. She dribbled nearly forty yards downfield before unleashing a shot. But goalkeeper Bente Norbdy made a spectacular save.

Mia didn't let the near miss slow her down. Just after the beginning of the second half, she slipped a pass by the Norwegian defense to Kristine Lilly. When Lilly saw that the goalie had committed herself, she passed the ball back to Mia. Mia nailed a left-footed shot into the right corner from twelve yards. The U.S. went on to win, 3–0, and Mia was named tournament MVP.

The team was playing well. If they kept on track, they could be unstoppable. But in a 2–1 victory over Japan in May, Mia pulled a hamstring behind her right knee. In the same game Tiffeny Milbrett strained a tendon in her foot.

Milbrett healed quickly, but Mia missed several games. She returned to action on June 25, 1998, in St. Louis, for a match with Germany. The Germans were still a strong team. Some observers were already calling them the favorite in the upcoming World Cup.

The Germans took a 1–0 lead. On defense, they focused on Mia. Each time she touched the ball, she was marked aggressively. Finally, in the fifty-sixth minute, German defender Steffi Jones received a yellow card after needlessly knocking Mia to the ground.

A few minutes later, Coach DiCicco pulled Mia from the game. Her hamstring had held up well, but he didn't want her to push it and get hurt. Fortunately, Cindy Parlow scored a few minutes later and the U.S. emerged with a 1–1 tie.

Three days later, the two teams played a rematch. Mia was determined not to allow the Germans to intimidate her.

At the half the Americans led, 1–0. Moments into the second half, Steffi Jones tried to clear the ball from the German end, but inadvertently stepped on the ball and fell down.

Now Mia got her revenge. She swooped in on the ball and moved in on a breakaway, rolling a shot past the goalie into the right corner from twelve yards.

Two minutes later, she struck again. Julie Foudy

stole a pass and fed Mia on the right side of the penalty box. Mia froze a German defender, then stuck a shot into the left corner to put the U.S. ahead, 3–0.

The Germans scored a goal soon after, but it wasn't going to be enough. With the score 3–1, Tiffeny Milbrett shed a defender and sent a perfect cross into the penalty area. Mia fought her way to the ball and booted it into the top of the net for a hat trick and her ninety-second international goal. Though the Germans managed to score once more, the Americans won, 4–2.

One month later, the team began competition in the Goodwill Games, played in the United States. The four teams in the tournament — Denmark, China, Norway, and the U.S. — were among the best in the world.

In the opening match, the U.S. played Denmark. After eighteen minutes without taking a shot, Mia and her teammates exploded. Mia took a pass from Kristine Lilly, then split the defenders by sending a return pass to Lilly. Lilly converted from ten yards to give the Americans a one-goal advantage. Michelle Akers added another goal a few minutes later.

The second half was Mia's time. With the help of her teammates and some expertly run offense, she scored a hat trick in her second consecutive game, giving her ninety-five career goals in 151 games and the Americans a 5–0 victory over Denmark.

The victory earned the Americans a spot in the finals against China, which defeated Norway in the other semifinal. Before the game Coach DiCicco told his team, "This is important with the World Cup being here [in the U.S.] next year. We don't want China, or any other team, to feel they can beat us here."

From the very beginning, the game was close. Of all the other teams in the world, China was perhaps the only one that could match the Americans' athleticism, speed, discipline, and intensity.

In the first half neither team was able to score. Mia was repeatedly hammered by the physical Chinese defense. Once, she crumpled to the ground when she was sandwiched by two Chinese defenders. Fortunately, she wasn't hurt.

In the sixty-sixth minute, the Americans finally found a seam in the Chinese defense. As the Chinese defense collapsed around Kristine Lilly on the right side, she passed the ball across to Mia. Mia gave it a quick touch, then spun it into the left side of the net. "I hit it as hard as I could," she said later. "Thank goodness it went in."

The goal hurt the Chinese team's confidence. Twenty minutes later, Debbie Keller forced China to make a poor clearing pass. Mia collected the free ball, spun, and sent in a booming shot from thirty-five yards out. The United States took a 2–0 lead. As soon as she scored, Mia ran the length of the field to the American bench, then slid on her knees in celebration before her cheering teammates.

"Mia turned in a Michael Jordan–like performance tonight," said Coach DiCicco after the 2–0 win.

"I thought before the game that she was the best player in the world," admitted Chinese goalkeeper Zho Yan after the game. "And I still feel that way."

After winning the gold medal in the Goodwill Games, Mia continued her assault on the record book. Against Mexico in September in the opening match of the Nike U.S. Women's Cup, she scored twice for her ninety-eighth and ninety-ninth career goals and collected a remarkable four assists as the U.S. won, 9–0.

In her next game, against Russia before 13,000 fans in Rochester, New York, Mia ran down a bouncing ball and ripped a volley high into the left side of the net for her one hundredth goal.

The game was stopped for several minutes as her teammates surrounded her and captain Carla Overbeck presented her with the ball.

"It was a fantastic night, certainly one that I will remember forever," she said. "The crowd was great and it was a lot of fun, but it was even better because I could share it with my teammates. It's a credit to this team that we can have moments like this."

She proved that the team was more important to her than personal glory in the finals against Brazil. Although Mia didn't score a goal, she collected two assists as the United States shut down Brazil, 3–0.

After the win, the team took some time off. When they gathered together again, it would be to begin final preparations for their real goal, the only one that really mattered to Mia and her teammates.

The 1999 Women's World Cup was approaching.

Chapter Thirteen:
1999

Return to the Cup

To prepare for the World Cup, the team went to training camp together in December. Coach DiCicco watched them all carefully and made his final roster decisions. Then the team embarked on an ambitious exhibition schedule to prepare for Cup competition and drum up public interest in the games.

Wherever the team went, Mia was the focus of attention. She was the most famous women's soccer player in the world, and for many people, the only soccer player they had ever heard of or could recognize. Wherever she went, she was mobbed by young fans and under intense pressure to play up to her usual standard. She didn't disappoint.

The record for most goals scored was well within reach. Mia tallied number 103 in the first match of the season against Portugal in a 7–0 win, and notched number 104 three days later in a rematch, another U.S. win. One month later she scored number 105 against Finland.

But when the United States team traveled to Portugal for the Algarve Cup, a tournament with the best European teams as well as China and Australia, Mia went into a slump. Although the American team won the tournament, she didn't score a single goal.

On one level, Mia really didn't care. As long as her team was winning, she was happy.

But on another level, she was concerned. Her teammates depended on her to score. She didn't want to let them down, and she didn't want to lose confidence before entering the World Cup.

Finally, on May 2 in Atlanta, Mia broke her slump by nailing a twenty-yard blast that bent around the Japanese goalkeeper. It was number 106 of her international career.

"I always want to score goals," she said later, "but the important thing is that we win. If I'm not putting the ball into the net, someone will step up to get the job done."

In the end, it was Mia who got the job done. On

May 22 against tough Brazil, she scored record-setting goal number 108. Now she could focus on helping her team win the World Cup.

Interest in the tournament continued to grow. One of the reasons was a series of commercials featuring members of the team. One showed Mia playing a variety of sports against Michael Jordan. Mia laughed when reporters asked her if she was actually able to keep up with Jordan, saying, "I have so much respect for him — you watch him play and you're speechless." Regardless, the commercial made the point that Mia was just as much an athlete as Jordan.

It was obvious that Mia had struck a positive chord when the team took the field on June 19, 1999, at the Meadowlands in New Jersey for the opening game of the World Cup against Denmark. The stadium was packed to capacity with more than 78,000 fans. Hundreds, maybe thousands of young soccer players, both male and female, wore replicas of Mia's signature number nine jersey. It was Mia-mania. They started cheering at the beginning of the match and kept it up the whole game.

Mia and her teammates didn't let them down. After a slow start with players on both teams fighting first-game jitters, the United States struck.

The United States had the ball. Mia streaked downfield, outrunning several pursuers who simply didn't have enough speed to keep up with her. Brandi Chastain booted a long pass to her on the right side, about fifteen yards from the net. Mia took the pass off her body, gained control, then went to work.

As defender Kristine Pedersen approached, Mia turned with the ball. She faked to the left, but Pedersen held her ground. So Mia faked right. Pedersen went for it.

As she did, Mia moved to her left again. The Danish goalkeeper was also mesmerized by her moves, and couldn't decide whether to come out and challenge Mia or to protect the goalmouth.

Mia took advantage of her indecision. Lightning quick, she shuffled the ball to her left foot and pounded a rocket toward the goal. The goalkeeper made a desperate dive, but the shot soared into the top of the net. The U.S. led, 1–0. Mia had scored the first goal of the World Cup!

The Danes couldn't keep up with her after that. For the rest of the match she ran them ragged.

But as the game entered its final twenty minutes, the U.S. still led just 1–0. They needed another goal to put the game away.

In the seventy-second minute, Mia threw the ball in from the right side. She followed the ball, and her teammate gave it back to her on a "give and go." Mia took control at the side of the penalty box. She was cut off from the goal, but spotted teammate Julie Foudy streaking down the opposite side.

Her long cross pass hit Foudy in midstride. Foudy knocked in the goal off the near post. The U.S. led, 2–0. A few moments later, they scored again and won the match, 3–0.

After the game, everyone was talking about Mia.

"Mia was awesome," Coach DiCicco said simply. Team cocaptain Julie Foudy agreed. "When she made that first goal," she said, "I think we were all like, 'Yeah, we're going to be okay.'"

Mia, of course, downplayed her role. "To tell the truth," she said afterward, "I don't remember it, but I was excited." Then, when a reporter asked her about the crowd and all the young players wearing her jersey, Mia lit up. "I feel good about that," she said. "When they leave the stadium, they want to play in the World Cup. That's what it was about."

In their next match, the U.S. faced Nigeria, a quick, athletic team they knew little about. More than 60,000 fans at Chicago's Soldier Field roared, but just two minutes into the match they were silenced. The Nigerians dramatically demonstrated that the favored Americans didn't intimidate them. They scored a goal to go ahead, 1–0.

For the next seventeen minutes, the inspired Nigerians played the U.S. to a standoff, playing Mia particularly close. Then Mia took command.

From the left sideline, she rocketed a kick off defender Ifeanyichukwu Chiejene. Michelle Akers dove toward the free ball and got her foot on it, deflecting it into the net to tie the game.

Less than a minute later, Mia struck again. She was left alone on the right wing and Kristine Lilly hit her on the run with a pass.

Goalkeeper Ann Chiejine was out of position. But when she saw Mia, the keeper started frantically backpedaling toward the goal. Too late. Mia kicked a rocket that sailed over Chiejine's head into the net to make the score 2–1.

Nigeria never recovered. The Americans rolled to a convincing 7–1 win. Then, in their final game of group play, the United States beat North Korea to make it to the final round. They were only three wins away from winning the World Cup.

They faced the tough Germans in the quarter-finals. From the beginning of the match, the Germans made it clear that they intended to do everything they could to stop Mia.

She was marked roughly, and when the U.S. allowed an own goal only five minutes into the match as Brandi Chastain booted the ball past goalie Briana Scurry, the U.S. trailed, 1–0. Though the U.S. managed to score a goal, the Germans kept the pressure on, and scored again just before halftime to take a 2–1 lead.

The Americans regrouped. Mia led the comeback. Four minutes into the second half, with the U.S. on attack, the ball rolled past the endline, setting up a corner kick. Mia placed the ball on the ground and prepared to kick, surveying the players grouped before the goal.

She paused for a moment to gather herself, then arched a twisting shot in front of the goal. Brandi

Chastain made up for her earlier error by fighting her way through a crowd and sending a header into the net to tie the game.

Now the United States had momentum. Twenty-one minutes later, the U.S. scored the game-winner when Joy Fawcett headed in another goal off a corner from Shannon MacMillan. The Americans held on to win, 3–2, to advance to the semifinals.

Only Brazil stood in their way to reaching the final. They met on the Fourth of July at Stanford University in California before another capacity crowd.

Like the Nigerians, whom they'd beaten to reach the final round, the Brazilians were a quick, athletic team. And like the Nigerians, they weren't intimidated.

The U.S. team may have been looking ahead to the final, and were caught off guard. All game long the Brazilians sent shot after shot toward American goalie Briana Scurry. But Scurry proved up to her task. She shut out the Brazilians, and the Americans won, 2–0.

The victory sent the Americans into the final against China, which had defeated Norway by a convincing score of 5–0 in the other semifinal. Both teams had a week to prepare for the final.

Mia was exhausted and needed the time to recharge. Although she hadn't scored since the second game of the tournament, she'd been the object of the defense and had worked hard. Against the Chinese she knew she'd have to play her best game.

Everyone in America was swept up in World Cup fever, and over 90,000 fans turned out at the Rose Bowl in Pasadena, California, for the game, the biggest crowd ever for a women's sporting event. Even before the game was played, Mia and her teammates had proved that women's sports could be successful. Now all they needed was a World Cup win to drive the point home.

The two teams were evenly matched. Each time either went on the attack, the defense collapsed and cleared the ball. Time and time again Mia raced downfield and tried to get open, but the tough Chinese defenders prevented her from scoring.

At the end of regulation play, the game was scoreless, and in the final minutes the U.S. team had lost Michelle Akers, who had to leave the game after being bumped in the head. The game entered a fifteen-minute overtime period. A single score, a so-called golden goal, would win the game.

In the first overtime, China nearly broke through on a corner, but Kristine Lilly headed the ball out of the goalmouth. Then another fifteen-minute period was played. Although the U.S. pressured the rapidly tiring Chinese, it, too, passed scoreless. After 120 minutes of exhausting play, the World Cup would have to be decided on penalty kicks.

In a penalty kick situation, each team selects five players who alternate taking single shots from a fixed place twelve yards from the goal. The goal-keeper cannot move until the ball is struck. Whichever team makes the most goals wins.

In women's soccer, it is very difficult to stop a penalty kick, simply because female goalies aren't big enough to cover the entire net. To stop a shot, they have to anticipate where the shot is going.

The Americans hadn't been involved in a penalty kick situation in four years. Mia didn't care to end a game that way, and had even admitted that she lacked confidence in penalty kick situations. But no one was surprised when Coach DiCicco selected Mia along with Carla Overbeck, Joy Fawcett,

Kristine Lilly, and Brandi Chastain to shoot for the United States.

The Chinese shot first and their first two players scored, as did Carla Overbeck and Joy Fawcett for the U.S. Then Liu Ying stepped up to challenge Briana Scurry.

Scurry guessed the Chinese woman would shoot to the right side of the goal. So she dove accordingly.

Thump! The ball ricocheted off her hands and away from the net. No goal! The score remained 2–2.

Kristine Lilly then scored to put the U.S. ahead, but seconds later another Chinese player beat Scurry to make it 3–3.

Now it was Mia's turn. If she scored, the Americans would move ahead.

She took a deep breath and approached the ball as 90,000 soccer fans cheered and millions more around the world watched on television. She knew this was the most important kick of her career.

She stood several yards behind the ball, concentrating. Then she took a few quick steps and kicked the ball with her right foot.

The ball went on a line just inside the right post. The Chinese goalkeeper tried in vain to stop it.

GOAL! The Americans led, 4–3. Mia ran over and collapsed into the arms of her teammates.

But, moments later, Chinese star Sun Wen tied the score. The game came down to a single kick by Brandi Chastain.

Without hesitation, Chastain drilled the ball into the corner of the net. The Americans had won!

In an instant she was engulfed by her teammates as the crowd roared and cheered and roared some more. Mia and her teammates had reached their goal. All their dreams had come true. Not only were they world champions, but they had made their sport a success. Young girls across the globe knew there was a place for them in sports.

"We came to understand," said Mia later, "that this World Cup wasn't just about us winning. This is a historic event far beyond any single result. If we lose sight of that, everything we did would be for nothing." As millions of young girls playing soccer around the world could tell you, Mia Hamm has never ever lost sight of what is most important.

The #1
Sports Writer
for Kids

MATT CHRISTOPHER

Read them all!

All available in paperback from Little, Brown and Company

Matt Christopher

Sports Bio Bookshelf